DANIEL
FROM START2FINISH

MICHAEL WHITWORTH

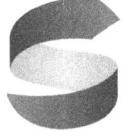

© 2015 by Start2Finish Books

All rights reserved. No part of this publication may be reproduced, stored in a retrieval system, or transmitted in any form or by any means without the prior written permission of the author. The only exception is brief quotations in printed reviews.

ISBN-10: 1941972780
ISBN-13: 978-1941972786

Published by Start2Finish Books
PO Box 660675 #54705
Dallas, TX 75266-0675
www.start2finish.org

Printed in the United States of America

Unless otherwise noted, all Scripture quotations are from The Holy Bible, English Standard Version®, copyright © 2001 by Crossway Bibles, a publishing ministry of Good News Publishers. Used by permission. All rights reserved.

Cover Design: Josh Feit, Evangela.com

CONTENTS

1. Daniel in Babylon (Dan. 1) — 5
2. The First Dream (Dan. 2:1-30) — 12
3. The Statue (Dan. 2:31-49) — 19
4. The Fiery Furnace (Dan. 3) — 28
5. The Second Dream (Dan. 4) — 37
6. Writing on the Wall (Dan. 5) — 46
7. The Lions' Den (Dan. 6) — 55
8. The Four Beasts (Dan. 7) — 63
9. The Ram & the Goat (Dan. 8) — 72
10. The Seventy Weeks (Dan. 9) — 83
11. The Vision (Dan. 10) — 92
12. The Script (Dan. 11) — 99
13. The End? (Dan. 12) — 110

1

DANIEL IN BABYLON
DANIEL 1

Objective: To affirm God's sovereignty and the importance of firm resolve in seasons of trial

INTRODUCTION

Anyone old enough to remember 9/11 will never forget that day. Americans that came of age in a post-Cold War world grew to believe, falsely, that America was untouchable. But the unthinkable happened when the World Trade Center towers collapsed. Disaster and disorientation ensued. Americans learned the hard way that the world had changed and that we were not invincible to our enemies.

The Book of Daniel opens with the collapse of a dream. For centuries, the nation of Israel also believed herself to be invincible to her enemies. God would always preserve his people, his city, and his Temple. But in 605 B.C., the unthinkable happened—Jerusalem was conquered by Nebuchadnezzar. Disaster and disorientation ensued, both of which can be a breeding ground for disappointment with God and rebellion against his will.

This is why Daniel's story is so remarkable. A young man separated from his parents, deported to an exotic land far away from his homeland, and offered whatever his heart could desire—the situation was ripe for rebellion against God. But Daniel knew God was still in control and thus resolved to obey him. He illustrates for us how to live faithfully in a culture hostile to faith and obedience.

EXAMINATION

Read Daniel 1:1-7. The story of Daniel opens with a historical note that Nebuchadnezzar successfully besieged Jerusalem and carried off captives as well as treasures from the Temple. It seemed as if the gods of Babylon had been victorious against Israel's God. But not so, the narrator claims. Rather, he emphasizes that the Lord had given Jerusalem into Nebuchadnezzar's hands. God was still in complete control of all things.

Daniel and his three friends were likely teenage members of the royal family in Jerusalem (cf. Isa. 39:7). The captives are said to have been "without blemish," a term often used in Leviticus of sacrifices. They were also "of good appearance," "skillful in all wisdom," etc. The narrator's point is that these were good-looking, very smart young men with great promise—the kind you'd want your daughter to marry.

Nebuchadnezzar chose to deport the elite young men of Jerusalem because it discouraged rebellion and indoctrinated future leaders of the Empire. As part of their training, they were allowed to eat and drink from the king's table, but they were also subjected to a daunting academic track designed to make them thoroughly Babylonian in every conceivable way. The curriculum required students to copy out texts in subjects such as math, science, literature, history, and religion.

Consistent with a very common practice of antiquity, the four captives received new names.

- "Daniel," meaning "God is my judge," became "Belteshazzar," meaning "Bel, protect his life!"
- "Hananiah" ("Yahweh is gracious") became "Shadrach" ("Command of Aku").
- "Mishael" ("Who is like God?") became "Meshach" ("Who is like Aku?").
- "Azariah" ("Yahweh has helped") became "Abednego" ("servant of Nego/Nebo," a variant of "Nabu").

Read Daniel 1:8-21. The word "resolved" in v. 8 is among the most important in the entire book. It marks Daniel as a man of great integrity and conviction, one absolutely committed to doing God's will and bringing God glory. One commentator calls Daniel's resolve an "outward sign of a determined loyalty." To avoid defiling himself, Daniel made an odd request.

This request was received semi-favorably because God had caused the official to show favor and compassion on Daniel (v. 9). Daniel's faithfulness did not necessarily earn him special treatment; rather, God mercifully orchestrated it so that Daniel's request was well received. The official explained his reluctance to accommodate Daniel's request since, if things went poorly, it would be off with the official's head (v. 10)! But Daniel spoke to the steward and arranged for only vegetables and water to be served for ten days.

Sure enough, at the end of the experiment, Daniel and his friends were in superior condition due to God's blessing. Not only did God grant them physical blessings, but also superior mental faculties, specifically the discerning ability "to accept what was true and to reject what was false in their instruction." Daniel was particularly given skill at understanding dreams, a detail prominently featured in subsequent stories. When Nebuchadnezzar inspected Daniel and his three friends, he found them "ten times better than" (or as we would say, "head and shoulders above") the rest of his royal wise men.

Finally, the statement that Daniel served in the palace until Cyrus' reign (v. 21) is more than a historical footnote. It testifies to Daniel's longevity. By God's grace, wise Daniel was able to navigate turbulent political waters successfully for nearly seven decades!

APPLICATION

Trust in God's Rule. The refrain of "God gave" in vv. 2, 9, 17 emphasizes that the Lord is in complete control at all times. This is the main theme of Daniel, as well as life's chief orienting principle. We do not submit to God's sovereignty while expecting him to bail us out of trouble; that isn't submission at all. But God has promised to exalt those who humble themselves before him, and he does so "in due time" (1 Pet. 5:6). The wise response to disaster or disorientation is to kneel before God's throne, confess him as "Lord," and resolve to honor him in all things. A God who was seemingly impotent at the beginning of the narrative when his Temple treasures were hauled away now had promoted four teenage boys above the most trusted advisors to Babylon's mighty monarch. God hadn't been defeated at all!

Be Salt & Light. It is interesting that the narrator does not object to Daniel and his friends being subjected to what amounted to brainwashing. Babylonian practices such as sorcery, astrology, and divination were forbidden under the Law of Moses (Deut. 18:10-14). We can only assume these four young men had a strong faith in God and were able to subject their education to God's wisdom (cf. 2 Cor. 10:5). The church needs leaders who have studied and understand culture so that we might engage in productive dialogue as Paul did in Athens. We must also be able to discern truth from error when the latter threatens Christ's body.

Resolve & Respect. We must show resolve when necessary, but doing so with dignity and respect is also important. Daniel was not rude or insulting—his request to abstain was respectful, and he was willing to seek a solution that satisfied all parties. Alexander Maclaren observed, "Many people seem to think that heroism is shown by rudeness." But Daniel modeled a different attitude, one of kindness and conviction, and he was successful (Prov. 22:11). Paul, too, warned that a strong faith and a martyr's spirit not tempered by love are both worthless (1 Cor. 13:2-3); we must treat everyone, even our ideological enemies, as precious souls created in God's image. It is important that as we stand for truth, we also check our attitudes and motives. Are we actually seeking to exalt God's principles—or our own glory?

CONCLUSION

It's easy to serve God faithfully while surrounded by other active Christians and when things are going well in life. But when disaster strikes—when we become disappointed and disoriented—Christians are tempted to rebel against the Lord and make things happen for ourselves. That's why we must remind ourselves regularly that God is in complete control. Christians also live in a world increasingly hostile to faith and obedience. It's easy to think that we have no choice but to "go with the flow." But Daniel's example of going against the current proves that success is found in resolve, not rebellion. If we trust God, he will take care of us (cf. Prov. 3:5-6). The Lord always provides for his people.

QUESTIONS FOR REFLECTION

1. What does the narrator emphasize in vv. 1-2?

2. How are Daniel and his friends described physically?

3. What does it mean that Daniel "resolved in his heart"?

4. Describe Daniel's attitude when he made his request.

5. How was God's power demonstrated in the story's end?

QUESTIONS FOR DISCUSSION

1. What is the proper response to disaster and disorientation?

2. Why is it important to confess often that God is in control?

3. What made it easier for Daniel to "go against the grain"?

4. Why is it often easier to rebel than resolve?

5. How can a Christian show resolve without being rude?

6. What implications does this story hold for Christian parents?

2

THE FIRST DREAM

DANIEL 2:1-30

Objective: To affirm God's knowledge and control of the future and encourage faith in the Lord's wisdom and power

INTRODUCTION

All of us wish we could know something about the future. If I could legitimately predict for you one detail about the future, wouldn't you be the least bit curious? What detail would it be? How much longer you'd live? The next hot stock? Next year's Super Bowl champion? In reality, none of us can predict the future (Jas. 4:14-15). Christians often say, "I don't know what the future holds, but I know who holds the future," and that's true. God has perfect knowledge of the future. This is the clear and consistent claim of Scripture, and it is the point of this story.

Whenever this chapter is discussed, much is said about the coming of God's kingdom. Rightly so, given the mention of the great stone and the eternal kingdom in v. 44. But the narrator of Daniel is less concerned with identifying historically each part of the statue and more concerned with exalting God as the only One with knowledge of and control over the future. The Aramaic terms translated "interpretation," "mystery," and "reveal" appear 13x, 8x, and 7x respectively in this chapter. In other words, this passage mentions the future advent of God's kingdom, but its chief concern is to exalt God as the fount of all wisdom and understanding, even of things that remain hidden—like the future! This is the refrain of Daniel: God knows the future. God is in control.

EXAMINATION

Read Daniel 2:1-16. It was common for ancient kings to have dreams. The ancient world considered dreams a very ordinary means for the gods to communicate with men. Here, God was communicating with Nebuchadnezzar by means he would accept although not completely understand.

An interesting note: beginning with the words "in Aramaic" (v. 4), the text switches from Hebrew to Aramaic until the end of Dan. 7. We are not told why, but it is commonly believed that the portions in Hebrew were of particular relevance to the Jews, while the section in Aramaic applied to everyone.

Babylonian dreamologists had sophisticated techniques for interpreting dreams; they had developed "dream manuals," which recorded various dreams and their appropriate interpretations based on past events. This is why the wise men were so insistent the king reveal his dream (vv. 4, 7, 10-11). But Nebuchadnezzar believed, and correctly so, that anyone posing as a dream-interpreter would be able to reveal the dream's details. The wise men were attempting delay tactics in hopes that the dream would come to pass and thus be easy to interpret.

When his wise men proved useless, the king matter-of-factly

told them, "Interpret my dream, or else…" The "or else" was an oath to dismember the entire group and turn their homes into public porta-potties (cf. 2 Kgs. 10:27). The final appeal of the wise men is very revealing: "There is not a man on earth who can meet the king's demand…no one can show it to the king except the gods." Indeed. And it would not be anyone on earth who would reveal the dream and its meaning, for only God in heaven can do that. Not only did the wise men unwittingly expose themselves as complete frauds, but the Holy Spirit puts the main point of the passage on their lips: God alone is the source of all wisdom, knowledge, and understanding.

As the guards went about rounding up the wise men for this mass (and presumably very public) execution, Daniel intervened. He requested an audience with Nebuchadnezzar so that he might explain the dream and its meaning. Bizarrely, the king gave Daniel the time he sought in spite of denying more time to the wise men and accusing them of stalling intentionally. God was clearly at work for Nebuchadnezzar to have done this very unexpected thing.

Read Daniel 2:17-30. Daniel returned to his residence and implored his three friends to join him in pleading prayer. Quite literally, they prayed like their lives depended on it! When God answered their prayer, Daniel offered up a prayer of thanksgiving with three important points.

- *The Lord is "the God of heaven,"* affirming that the God of the sun, moon, and stars had done what Babylon's pagan astrologers could not.
- *To God belong "wisdom and power."* God's people have no reason to go anywhere else to obtain wisdom and power, for God gives wisdom and knowledge, and he explains what is deep and hidden.
- *God's absolute sovereignty over the earth* is expressed in

how "he changes times and seasons," which means history bends to God's will. God always knows the future and controls its unfolding.

Daniel ended his prayer by again thanking God for answering his request to understand "the king's matter" (v. 23). Only after Daniel had received what he had requested and properly thanked God for the reply did he announce to Arioch his readiness to go before Nebuchadnezzar. In vv. 27-28, Daniel found a respectful way of telling the king that his pagan religion was a farce (cf. Isa. 41:21-24), and that the king wasn't all that special in the first place.

In the next lesson, we'll explore the meaning of the king's dream.

APPLICATION

Does God Know the Whole Future? Some teach that God has a limited knowledge of the future. Others contend that God is not involved with the unfolding of future events. But both of these views are without biblical basis. Rather, God has a plan, and he shapes events to ensure his plan unfolds perfectly (Acts 2). Nothing ever happens that God does not anticipate. Nothing can hijack his purposes (Job 42:2). Such a fact can be both disconcerting and comforting. Disconcerting because it will sometimes prompt us to ask why an omniscient, omnibenevolent God could allow bad things to happen; comforting because faith inspires us to profess that he will allow nothing to happen unless it's for our good and his glory. Whenever God's people feel afflicted, oppressed, endangered, or on death's doorstep, remember that God is the source of all wisdom and power. Nothing can happen to his people that he has not thoroughly thought through from beginning to end (Isa. 46:10), and he can intervene at any time and in any way consistent with his good will.

Prayer: Our First Line of Defense. It is significant that, as soon as he knew his life was in danger, Daniel prayed. As it was for Daniel, prayer should be our first line of defense. A. W. Tozer once wrote, "Whatever God can do faith can do, and whatever faith can do prayer can do when it is offered in faith. An invitation to prayer is, therefore, an invitation to omnipotence, for prayer engages the Omnipotent God and brings Him into our human affairs. Nothing is impossible to the man who prays in faith, just as nothing is impossible with God." Prayer is never a last resort (e.g. "All we can do now is pray!") but is the most potent weapon in the Christian arsenal.

Humility Under Fire. When he gave Nebuchadnezzar the dream's interpretation, Daniel demonstrated remarkable humility. He was qualified to give the interpretation, not because he was more talented or gifted than the king's other servants, but because Daniel was God's chosen vessel. This fact humbled Daniel and prompted him to trust the Lord even more. His example reminds us that personal talents and abilities matter less than our humble willingness to be used by God for his glory. As it is often put, God does not call the qualified; he qualifies the called. Whenever we do great things for God, let us remember that such was not possible without the Lord's blessing and power.

CONCLUSION

None of us knows the future, but we have the incredible opportunity to trust in the One who does. The king's wise men proved themselves frauds when it came to unraveling mysteries. But Daniel demonstrated great faith by asking the Lord to reveal the dream and its meaning to him. Instead of seeking to secure ourselves a better future by our own ingenuity, let us continue to trust and obey the Lord in all things, for he alone knows what lies ahead.

LESSON 2: THE FIRST DREAM • 17

QUESTIONS FOR REFLECTION

1. Why were the king's wise men so insistent that Nebuchadnezzar share the details of his dream?

2. What great biblical truth does the Holy Spirit put on the lips of the wise men?

3. What was the king's response to Daniel's request for more time? Why was this significant?

4. What did Daniel do once he returned from requesting more time to interpret the dream?

5. What three characteristics of God did Daniel emphasize in his prayer of thanksgiving?

QUESTIONS FOR DISCUSSION

1. Do you believe God knows the future? Why/why not?

2. How does his foreknowledge both frustrate and comfort us?

3. Why is prayer the most potent weapon in our arsenal? Rather than pray, how do some Christians react to trials?

4. How are Christians often guilty of trusting in their own wisdom and power and not the Lord's?

5. How does faith inspire us to act when we are, on our own, not qualified for the task or trial before us?

3

THE STATUE

DANIEL 2:31-49

Objective: To explore God's eternal plan for his people and to celebrate its fulfillment

INTRODUCTION

In the previous lesson, we discovered that God is in control of the future and that he alone has the power to reveal it to his servants. Instead of the king's wise men, Daniel was granted knowledge of Nebuchadnezzar's dream and its interpretation. Daniel then went to the king with bold humility and explained the dream to him.

In the second part of Dan. 2, we are given a glimpse of what God had been plotting for the good of his people since before the foundations of the world (Tit. 1:2). The entire Old Testament story was destined to climax with the coming of Christ and the establishment of the church. Mighty as he was, Nebuchadnezzar was just a supporting actor in God's universal, timeless drama. Unlike the empires of Babylon, Persia, Greece, and Rome, the Lord of heaven was planning to establish a kingdom that would never pass away.

EXAMINATION

Read Daniel 2:31-45. In Nebuchadnezzar's dream, he saw a great statue, one that inspired both awe and fear. It was comprised of various metals, each less precious but more unbreakable than the previous one—until we come to the feet. A stone "cut out by no human hand" (v. 34) shattered the statue's feet, at which point the entire thing was pulverized into smithereens and blew away without a trace. Meanwhile, "the stone that struck the image became a great mountain and filled the whole earth" (v. 35).

The text does not explicitly identify any part of the statue with a particular empire, except the head of gold—it was equal to Nebuchadnezzar's reign and, more broadly, the Babylonian Empire. Being the head of gold confirmed that Nebuchadnezzar ruled a great, majestic kingdom. But Daniel also reminded the king that his kingdom was a stewardship from God—it had been given to him by a superior, and the kingdom would be taken away and given to another. After Nebuchadnezzar, three more kingdoms would come—one of silver and the next of bronze. The fourth kingdom, one of iron, would be more destructive than the previous empires, but it would also be partly stronger and partly weaker.

The declining value of each empire suggests the human condition is worsening over time rather than improving. Note that, during the time of the fourth kingdom, "the God of heaven will set up a kingdom that shall never be destroyed, nor shall the kingdom be left to another people. It shall break in pieces all these kingdoms and bring them to an end, and it shall stand forever" (v. 44).

Until recent times, the overwhelming majority of interpreters considered these four kingdoms to be Babylon, Media-Persia, Greece, and Rome, respectively. This has been the historical interpretation, and there is evidence to support it, but questions remain.

Regardless of which empire matches which part of the statue, we can be certain of one thing: the identity of the stone. Ironically, the stone is never interpreted by Daniel, but as Augustine asked rhetorically, "Is not this rock Christ, which was cut without hands out of a mountain, from the kingdom of the Jews, without a husband's activity? Did not that stone break all the kingdoms of the world, that is, all the despotisms of idols and demons? Did not that stone grow and become a great mountain and fill the whole world?"

In Psalms, God is constantly alluded to as a "rock," so it is no stretch to identify Jesus—God in the flesh (John 1:14) and God with us (Matt. 1:23)—as that stone. The psalmist prophesied that God's Son would dash the nations to pieces (Psa. 2:9) just as the stone destroyed the statue. Jesus is "the stone that the builders rejected" yet became the cornerstone, and "everyone who falls on that stone will be broken to pieces, and when it falls on anyone, it will crush him" (Luke 20:17-18). It is not insignificant that this single prophecy, one that originated in Psa. 118:22, is among the most echoed in the New Testament (Matt. 21:42; Acts 4:11; 1 Pet. 2:7).

More than the stone, Jesus is the mystery that God patiently waited so long to reveal. His time on earth was known as the "last days" (Heb. 1:2). He embodies God's grand plan "to unite all things … in heaven and things on earth" (Eph. 1:9-10). He is "the mystery hidden for ages and generations but now revealed to his saints" (Col. 1:26). All of history was leading up to the coming of Christ and the establishment of the church.

Read Daniel 2:46-49. Nebuchadnezzar was so overwhelmed with gratitude for Daniel's service that he "paid homage" (cf. "honor" NIV) to the prophet. But this outburst of praise from Nebuchadnezzar did not signal his conversion. Nebuchadnezzar had a long way to go before his heart totally submitted to the God of heaven.

The king remained true to his original promise (v. 6) and rewarded Daniel greatly. He became the ruler over the entire province of Babylon, as well as head of the wise men, yet he was stationed in the king's court where he was always at the king's beck and call. Daniel's three friends (who feature prominently in the subsequent story) were also promoted.

What hope the Jews must have felt in their souls whenever they read this story! What was God thinking when he allowed Jerusalem to be destroyed? Did he have a plan in all this? Did the death of a dream mean the death of the promises of God? Had Israel been flung to the trash heap of history, doomed to eternal irrelevance? No. God still had a plan that he was working out, and he chose to reveal it in this dream to Nebuchadnezzar through Daniel.

APPLICATION

Lasting Security. Militaries lose; infrastructures fail; banking systems crash; nations collapse. The U.S. at one point did not exist, and—just like Babylon, Greece, and Rome—it too will eventually cease to exist. A key point of Nebuchadnezzar's dream is that nations built with human hands fail, but the kingdom made "without hands" (vv. 44-45) by God will stand forever. When Jesus came to earth, that kingdom was so close at hand that many in his generation would live to see it (Mark 1:15; 9:1). The kingdom of Christ was built "without hands" (cf. John 6:15; 18:36), with Jesus seated on David's throne in heaven (Acts 2:30). The moment a penitent believer is immersed with Christ in baptism, that person is automatically transferred into the Lord's kingdom (Col. 1:13). At that point, our spiritual citizenship is in heaven (Phil. 3:20). So long as we are part of this kingdom, the church (cf. Matt. 16:18), we are totally secure from even the most formidable of foes (Rom. 8:38-39). What a glorious kingdom!

False Security. King Nebuchadnezzar listened as Daniel interpreted his dream, something all the "wise men, enchanters, magicians, or astrologers" were unable to do (v. 27). In one of the most amazing examples of prophecy in all the Bible, Daniel vividly illustrated that there is a God in heaven (v. 28) who is sovereign over all nations (vv. 31-43) and will one day establish an everlasting kingdom (vv. 44-45). What is remarkable is Nebuchadnezzar's response. Astonishingly, he did not ask any questions about the future or inquire about Daniel's God who gave Daniel this incredible glimpse into the future. He did not ask about the meaning of life or the purpose of his existence. He did not repent of his wickedness or give up his idolatry. He was content knowing that he represented the golden head of the statue and that his fears of immediate trouble were groundless. In other words, Nebuchadnezzar was comfortable with his temporal little kingdom, and did not care about his future before the sovereign God of the universe. Like Nebuchadnezzar, we also put our trust in the wrong things at times, creating a false security. The only true security is found in the Lord (Jer. 9:23-24).

Intentional Influence. The Lord placed Daniel in the court of one of the most powerful rulers in history to be a testimony to the power of God. The Lord uses his people to give an answer to those within our sphere of influence (Jude 22; 2 Tim. 2:15; 1 Pet. 3:15). Accept the fact that you have influence over people around you. Are you being intentional about being a good influence? Additionally, are you being intentional about surrounding yourself with good influences? Daniel requested that the king appoint Shadrach, Meshach, and Abednego to help him with the affairs of the kingdom. He made it a point to surround himself with godly men. We draw strength from others (1 Cor. 15:33; Exod. 23:2). Be the kind of person around whom it is easy to be good. And choose friends around whom it is easy to be good.

CONCLUSION

Regardless of whether the four kingdoms of Dan. 2 should be identified as Babylon, Media-Persia, Greece, and Rome, God used all four to usher in "the fullness of time" (cf. Gal. 4:4). Because of the Babylonian exile, the Jewish synagogue was created, which Paul took advantage of to spread the gospel. The Persians contributed a deep respect for the rule of law, and the Greeks lent their language that became the common tongue of the first-century world. Finally, Pax Romana provided easy travel and Roman citizenship to Paul, which allowed him to take the gospel all the way to the capital city. After making these observations, Rex Turner concludes, "The Roman Empire unwittingly provided a cradle or protectorate for the infant church." All this came to pass by the perfect plan of God!

This gives me hope and strength to face the unknown future. Dark days may lie ahead for the church, but God has perfect knowledge of the future, and he will thus use future events, whether good or bad, to bring himself glory and bless his church. After all, the climax of history has been Christ and the church.

QUESTIONS FOR REFLECTION

1. Why did the statue inspire awe and fear in Nebuchadnezzar?

2. What did the declining value of each part of the statue (e.g. gold, silver, bronze, iron) represent?

3. Whom did the stone in v. 34 represent?

4. How did Christ and the church fulfill God's plan?

5. In what ways do you need to trust God more with the future?

QUESTIONS FOR DISCUSSION

1. In what ways do God's people put too much trust in the empires or kingdoms of today? Why is this trust misplaced?

2. Why is Christ more worthy of the church's trust?

3. In what ways does your congregation betray its conviction that God's kingdom might pass away?

4. How can your congregation trust Jesus more concerning the future?

5. What hope did this story give to the Jews who first read it?

6. How can you be more responsible with your influence in the world?

4

THE FIERY FURNACE

DANIEL 3

Objective: To illustrate the importance of obedience to God regardless of the circumstances

INTRODUCTION

Many of us learned the stories of Daniel as small children, particularly Daniel in the lions' den, as well as this story, the Fiery Furnace. But these stories' popularity with children may rob them of their frightening nature, leading us to conclude mistakenly that they don't merit serious consideration. When did you last appreciate the fact that in this story, three men opted to be burned alive rather than abandon their faith?

To be burned alive was an excruciating prospect. Families of the condemned often had green wood thrown on the flames so that the victim would die first of smoke inhalation before the flames could do their worst. This story in Dan. 3 is for a mature audience if there ever was one, and relegating it to children's Sunday school only injects the narrative with an inappropriate innocence.

Despite this story's happy ending, we cannot expect God to deliver us from every trial, tear, or terror. But this story does affirm for us that God is always with us in our suffering.

EXAMINATION

Read Daniel 3:1-7. In late 595-early 594 B.C., a revolt against Nebuchadnezzar took place, and the Fiery Furnace episode took place sometime the following year. Nebuchadnezzar likely intended this event to be a state-sponsored "celebration" of national unity, forcing members of his administration to take an oath of loyalty. At a place called the plain of Dura, Nebuchadnezzar gathered a long list of political leaders and cabinet members to commemorate the inaugural use of his statue. It was a pathetic ploy to solidify power and foster unity in the wake of a revolt. Surely, if there is a grand ceremony in which everyone does the same thing, there will no longer be rivalry and bitterness! Fallen humanity can have a very convoluted sense of unity.

Nebuchadnezzar's statue might have been inspired partly by the dream he had less than a decade prior in which he was depicted as a head of gold atop a massive statue. Thus he decided to erect one very similar to it. The image "of gold" stood ninety feet high by nine feet wide (cf. the Statue of Liberty at 151 feet).

The penalty for not worshipping the statue was being thrown into a "burning fiery furnace." This fiery furnace was likely shaped like a beehive and made of metal. It had an opening at the top so that the men could be tossed into it, and a door on the side (for adding fuel) with perhaps a window so that one could look in. It was certainly large enough to walk around in, as we will later see, and it could reach a temperature in excess of 1500°F. It was as convenient a means of execution as it was cruel; used to smelt the metal for the statue, Nebuchadnezzar likely repurposed it for destruction once its creative task was complete.

Read Daniel 3:8-18. Certain astrologers and wise men from the king's court—probably still smarting over these captives from Judah having been promoted above them—"maliciously accused the Jews." They reminded the king of his decree, and that his three provincial overseers were guilty of non-compliance. Nebuchadnezzar flew into a "furious rage" when he heard this.

He summoned the three men and, for some inexplicable reason, was willing to give them the opportunity for a change of heart. Was Nebuchadnezzar fond enough of them to extend a second chance? Or was he simply reluctant to lose such valuable administrators over a "misunderstanding"? We can't know. But by extending this second chance, Nebuchadnezzar provided the opportunity for a bold declaration of faith. The king's statement ended with an ill-advised dare.

The reply of Shadrach, Meshach, and Abednego is among the boldest statements in Scripture. It stands out, not only for its resolve, but also for its submission to God's sovereignty. Rather than reconsider, they opted to resign themselves to God's most perfect will. Nowhere in their statement did they express a belief in the afterlife, nor did they consider the consequence of their stand as reason to reconsider. No, these three men stood on little else than their love for the true God. They believed God could save them, but they never demanded he do so. If he saves, fine; if he doesn't, fine.

Read Daniel 3:19-30. Their response sent Nebuchadnezzar into a violent rage once again. The order came to heat the furnace "seven times hotter," likely accomplished with additional air and fuel. It would have been technically impossible even to double the furnace's temperature back then, let alone make it seven times hotter. The phrase is thus hyperbole, meaning something along the lines of "as hot as possible."

The king's "mighty men" (likely war veterans who had distinguished themselves in combat) bound and threw them into the furnace. They didn't even take the time to strip Shadrach, Meshach, and Abednego of their clothes, meaning they would have caught fire more quickly. The scene becomes more abhorrent when the king's henchmen were killed by the severe heat as they threw them in.

"Then King Nebuchadnezzar was astonished" (v. 24). *Surely, my eyes deceive me*, he apparently thought. As he gazed into the conflagration to witness the suffering of his rebellious administrators, he noticed they were no longer bound. Moreover, they were unharmed and walking around, and there was a fourth person with them in the furnace, one whose "appearance" was "like a son of the gods."

Throughout the OT, we are told that fire represents the divine presence (e.g. Exod. 3:2; 13:21; 24:17), and that fire cannot help but praise the Lord (Psa. 148:8). Nebuchadnezzar foolishly thought that casting these Israelites into the fire would put them beyond their God's ability to save. But the Lord of heaven, whose very presence is inside the fire and makes even the flames to praise him, demonstrated his complete sovereignty over the flames.

There is no place where we can escape God's presence (Psa. 139:7-12), nothing can separate us from his love (Rom. 8:38-39) or his deliverance (Psa. 68:20), and we have no reason to fear death itself since he has promised to personally lead us across the River (Psa. 48:14). As countless other martyrs have discovered through the ages, God is always present in the furnace of affliction.

When the three men walked out of the furnace, the power of God's miraculous deliverance was demonstrated in that their hair was not singed, their clothes were not burned, and they didn't even reek of smoke. The story ends with the king praising their courage and resolve not to dishonor their God by committing idolatry, and he gave all three a promotion. Nebuchadnezzar's words were laced with more than a little fear at the notion of having offended so powerful a God. The king went so far as to decree that those who blasphemed this God would be dismembered and their homes "renovated" into a latrine. But Nebuchadnezzar was not yet totally and exclusively converted to the worship of Yahweh. God and Nebuchadnezzar had a few more rounds to go.

APPLICATION

Thou Shalt Not Worship Other Gods. The tension of this passage is that everyone present was being compelled by the king to commit idolatry, something no Torah-loving Jew would have done. The Old Testament is replete with declarations that Yahweh is the only God (e.g. Isa. 43:10-13; 45:5-6, 18, 21-22). Moreover, idolatry was the reason Judah had been sent into exile in the first place (e.g. Isa. 30:19-22; Jer. 8:19; Ezek. 6:1-10), so the very thought of worshipping a false god would have been more than these three Hebrews could stomach. It's sadly too easy to fall into the trap of idolatry, and when trials come, our idols prove pathetically inadequate at delivering us. Thus, for those who truly love the Lord, showing worship and honor to anyone/thing else is simply unfathomable.

Thou Shalt Not Taunt God. Nebuchadnezzar's rhetorical question, "Who is the god who will deliver you out of my hands?" (v. 15) was a taunt that the Hebrew God was too impotent to do anything. One has to imagine God on his throne rolling his eyes when he heard those words. I'm not the smartest theologian in the world, but I know enough to know you don't taunt God's ability to deliver his people—"See now that I, even I, am he, and there is no god beside me; I kill and I make alive; I wound and I heal; and there is none that can deliver out of my hand" (Deut. 32:39). Pharaoh and Sennacherib made similar boasts (Exod. 5:2; 2 Kgs. 18:35; 19:12-13), yet the God of heaven humiliated both of them (Exod. 14:28; 2 Kgs. 19:35-37). Whenever the wicked mock God's power to save, we can rest assured that the Lord will do wondrous things to glorify himself.

Thou Shalt Believe in God's Power. Shadrach, Meshach, and Abednego were resolved together to reject worship of any god but Yahweh. They were emboldened to make such a radical confession by the tales they had heard of God's mightiest deeds. No amount of Babylonian brainwashing could make them forget how he had created the world from nothing, nor could they forget the Egyptian plagues and the Red Sea, Goliath's doom at Elah, and Elijah's victory on Carmel. They knew the mighty acts of Yahweh and were convinced beyond all doubt that God could be as powerful then as he had been in centuries past. When threatened, God's people must rehearse past demonstrations of his divine power lest they succumb to fear and do something motivated by doubt (cf. 2 Tim. 1:7).

DIGGING DEEPER

Who was the mysterious fourth person in the Fiery Furnace? Though the KJV says this one was like "the Son of God," the Aramaic is better translated as "son of the gods."

An angel. It's difficult to imagine a pagan Old Testament king claiming to see the New Testament Jesus in the flames. Jewish rabbis in the Talmud claimed this person was Gabriel the angel, and Nebuchadnezzar actually confessed later on that (from his perspective) God had "sent his angel" (v. 28). Even conservative scholars are hesitant to equate this fourth person with the pre-incarnate Christ.

Christ. The traditional interpretation of this fourth person is that it was the pre-incarnate Christ. To say that Nebuchadnezzar would not have recognized him as the Son of God is to miss the point. A pagan king would not have had perfect knowledge of God's nature, and may have in fact spoken greater truth than he knew.

In the end, the bigger point to be pressed is that God, in some form, was with these men in their suffering. He did not deliver them *from* the fire, but *in* the fire. Regardless of who this fourth person was, Christ is known to us as Immanuel, "God with us" (Matt. 1:23), and he has promised to never abandon us (Matt. 28:20, 2 Tim. 2:13).

CONCLUSION

Prudence might have demanded that these three Hebrews should have simply given in to Nebuchadnezzar's demands and bowed before the statue. Their external conformity did not have to affect their inner loyalty. Too often, we worry about the circumstances of obedience, rather than doing God's will and leaving the circumstances to him.

But Shadrach, Meshach, and Abednego demonstrate the importance of acting faithfully and entrusting ourselves to God's hand. He might not deliver us from every tyrant or trial, but he has sworn a solemn oath to be with us always, even in the furnace of affliction. God's people can endure every trial knowing he will never abandon us.

QUESTIONS FOR REFLECTION

1. Why did Nebuchadnezzar host this ceremony? What might have been the inspiration for the statue itself?

2. Why did Nebuchadnezzar give the three Hebrews a second chance to worship the statue? How did this second chance provide drama for the story?

3. What does it mean that the furnace was heated "seven times hotter"?

4. What does fire often symbolize in Scripture?

5. Whom do you believe to have been the fourth person?

6. When they emerged from the fiery furnace, how was the totality of God's deliverance demonstrated to the onlookers?

QUESTIONS FOR DISCUSSION

1. How did the response of the three Hebrews demonstrate both resolve and submission to God's will?

2. Regardless of his identity, what is the point of the fourth person present in the flames?

3. In commenting on this passage, Charles Spurgeon wrote, "Duties are ours, events are the Lord's." What does this statement mean to you? Do you agree with it?

4. When God's power is mocked by the wicked, what expectation or hope does this give Christians?

5. Why is God's presence more precious than his deliverance?

5

THE SECOND DREAM
DANIEL 4

Objective: To discuss the importance of dying to self and submitting to God as Lord of all

INTRODUCTION

In his famous book, *The Cost of Discipleship*, Dietrich Bonhoeffer wrote, "When Christ calls a man, he bids him come and die." That quote is a restatement of Jesus' call, "If anyone would come after me, let him deny himself and take up his cross daily and follow me" (Luke 9:23). Paul put it another way: "I have been crucified with Christ. It is no longer I who live, but Christ who lives in me" (Gal. 2:20).

Pride is deeply rooted in all of us, since few of us are very willing to admit that it is a problem. C. S. Lewis said there is no other sin of which we are more unconscious in ourselves. In his autobiography, Benjamin Franklin wrote, "In reality, there is, perhaps, no one of our national passions so hard to subdue as pride. Disguise it, struggle with it, beat it down, stifle it, mortify it as much as one pleases, it is still alive … even if I could conceive that I had completely overcome it, I should probably be proud of my humility."

So far, Nebuchadnezzar had witnessed God's ability to make known the future and protect his servants from the power of fire. But he had yet to die to self and kneel submissively before God. If the Lord cannot have the whole man, then he is uninterested in everything else about us. The king believed himself to be the captain of his own fate and the engine of his own prosperity. In so doing, he lost his mind and his kingdom; both were restored only when he turned "to heaven" (v. 34). For us, this story is a powerful reminder that we cannot inherit heaven's kingdom without bowing before God's throne.

EXAMINATION

Read Daniel 4:1-9. Some scholars have a hard time believing the events of this chapter. They are incredulous at the thought of a pagan king converting to the worship of the true God, and they allege that the account of Nebuchadnezzar losing his mind is a distortion of something that actually happened to a latter king of Babylon, Nabonidus. While there is no historical corroboration of this proclamation, nor of a seven-year absence during Nebuchadnezzar's reign, the fact is we know virtually nothing about the king's final thirty years. All we have from this part of Nebuchadnezzar's life is the biblical record, so this story would obviously sound fishy to anyone already prejudiced against God's Word.

This story likely takes place near the end of Nebuchadnezzar's life since the bulk of his building program had been completed (v. 30). He had retired from the field of battle, and he was enjoying the peaceful years of his reign now that his Empire dominated the known world. But during this season of life, the king had another dream. He called for his wise men and told them the dream (unlike the first time), but they were again useless to explain it. Daniel's delayed arrival (v. 8) gave the king another opportunity to witness the ineptness of his wise men.

Read Daniel 4:10-18. In the dream, the king saw a towering tree, "visible to the end of the whole earth" (v. 11). The tree provided food and shelter; Nebuchadnezzar is later identified with the tree, meaning the king saw himself as the "keeper of the cosmos," a title only God can rightfully claim (Col. 1:17). After the tree is described, an angel descended from heaven and called for the tree to be chopped down, its branches hewn, and its leaves and fruit scattered. Its stump and roots, however, were to remain; the stump would be preserved with a band of iron and bronze. Meanwhile, Nebuchadnezzar would eat grass like an ox and lose his mind for "seven periods of time." This decree from the watcher was given so "that the living may know that the Most High rules the kingdom of men and gives it to whom he will and sets over it the lowliest of men" (v. 17).

Read Daniel 4:19-27. Daniel seemed to know immediately the significance of the king's dream. As it had the king, the dream "alarmed him" (v. 19), but he was also embarrassed and was speechless for a brief while. Daniel's affection for the king is evident in his wish that the dream apply to Nebuchadnezzar's enemies, but Daniel knew better. As he explained, the tree represented Nebuchadnezzar. The king had become strong and great, but the "decree of the Most High" via the angel was that he would be driven from civilization and into the wild. This would be for "seven periods of time" until the king confessed "that the Most High rules the kingdom of men and gives it to whom he will" (v. 25). While he was away, his kingdom would be preserved for him. At the end of the dream's explanation, Daniel begged Nebuchadnezzar to act preemptively so that the dream would not come to pass. Specifically, Nebuchadnezzar was exhorted to "break off" his sin by "practicing righteousness." After all, Prov. 29:14 says, "If a king judges poor people fairly, his government will continue forever." The king had not exhibited such kindness and justice to the disenfranchised of his Empire.

Read Daniel 4:28-37. Nebuchadnezzar is remembered by historians, not only for his success as a military leader, but also for his accomplishments as a builder. Many of the bricks used in Nebuchadnezzar's building programs were stamped with his name. He constructed canals so that the Euphrates River flowed through the city, docks to service ships and passengers, and a 400-foot-long bridge across the Euphrates, connecting the east and west portions of Babylon. He commissioned the Hanging Gardens of Babylon as a gift for his wife. With its lush plants, waterfalls, and orchards, the Hanging Gardens were the first of Babylon's two entries to the Seven Wonders of the Ancient World. Its city walls were the second. The outer wall alone was nearly seventeen miles long, forty feet high, 25 feet thick, and "wide enough at the top for chariots to pass."

It's been said, "It's not bragging if it's true." Nebuchadnezzar's words were true, yet they were also boastful and arrogant before the Most High. No sooner had Nebuchadnezzar bragged about his magnificent accomplishments than the judgment in his dream rang out from heaven (vv. 31-32). Nebuchadnezzar was driven away from civilization, ate and lived like a cow, his body drenched with dew, and his hair and nails grew to resemble a bird's feathers and claws. Being exposed to the elements would have been horrible—temperatures in that area of the world can soar into the triple digits during the summer and drop below freezing in the winter.

Throughout the chapter, there is repeated mention of "seven periods of time" as the duration of Nebuchadnezzar's punishment. Almost every interpreter has understood this to mean seven years. But I agree with Homer Hailey, who sees seven times as symbolic of perfection and completion, "an indefinite time for the complete accomplishment of a divine purpose." He argues that this was an indefinite period lasting until Nebuchadnezzar finally acknowledged

God's sovereignty. This is corroborated in vv. 17, 25, 32 and by the phrase "at the end of the days" (v. 34).

Nebuchadnezzar had his empire and power restored to him, but only after he had knelt in submission before God. In his doxology, he acknowledged, "All the inhabitants of the earth are accounted as nothing." This does not mean God is unconcerned with us, but that the greatest of men have as much chance of dethroning God as an ant has against my boot.

APPLICATION

The King of Kings. Scripture is clear that God raises up rulers and gives them power as a stewardship. Though rulers have free will, God nonetheless can manipulate them according to his purposes (Prov. 21:1). Simply put, it is God's prerogative to establish people in positions of authority at any time for any reason. Schemes, plots, coups, and elections make it seem as if we are responsible for our own leaders, but the Bible maintains a different reality. When Christians are subject to a righteous ruler, we should praise God for that blessing; when we are subject to a wicked ruler, we can pray for deliverance, but we must never conclude that God "has messed up" or fallen asleep at the wheel. When he raises up wicked rulers, God will use them to glorify himself and bless his people, even if in disguise.

Practice Righteousness. Nebuchadnezzar was encouraged to prevent or delay the judgment of the dream by practicing righteousness (i.e. showing kindness to the downtrodden). Some Christians attempt in vain to segment their spiritual life from the physical, pretending that their relationship with God is disconnected from their relationship with others. But the New Testament is clear that a healthy relationship with God is defined in part by our concern for "the least of these" (Matt 25:31-46; Jas. 1:27). Even in Mic. 6:8, God reminded Israel that what he desired, even more than ritual sacrifices and external obedience to worship regulations, was a heart that sought justice, loved mercy, and walked humbly with God. Indeed, showing kindness to "the least of these" helps us maintain heaven's perspective in life—namely, that we would be no better than they if it were not for the very amazing grace of God. The alternative—believing that success and comfort in life are our own accomplishments—will make us literally lose our minds in God's eyes.

Look to Heaven. There is something to be said for Nebuchadnezzar's sudden return to reason when he turned his gaze to heaven. We are never less in our right mind than when our pride controls us. It was pride that drove a young man to brazenly request his inheritance while his father was still living. So starved that he was eating pig slop, "he came to himself" (Luke 15:17) and realized his father's slaves lived like kings compared to his present circumstances. If you think through dark seasons of your life, you will notice that things might have been going well externally, but your inner person had no joy because your pride was reigning in the place of God. On the other hand, how many people have we known that endured terrible circumstances externally, but were filled with an internal joy because they had died to self and looked to heaven for guidance?

CONCLUSION

It's not enough to modify our behavior to appear more humble; we must ruthlessly and regularly put our pride to death. Maybe our tree needs to fall so that we can abandon ourselves to another tree, a cross that births glory out of shame. "When Christ calls a man, he bids him come and die," for Christ cannot bring us eternal life as long as our pride is alive and working for our destruction. But the very moment we die to self and take up the King's tree, we become heirs of a kingdom far greater than any on earth.

There is a message of hope in the fact that Nebuchadnezzar—though forced to live in the wild and vulnerable to all that could happen in such circumstances—still fell under the protection of heaven. God had promised to preserve his throne, and he did so. On how many occasions has God preserved our lives so that we might finally turn our hearts to him in faith and obedience? "Or do you presume on the riches of his kindness and forbearance and patience, not knowing that God's kindness is meant to lead you to repentance?" (Rom. 2:4). Live not another moment without dying to self and discovering the grace of life as a servant of King Jesus!

QUESTIONS FOR REFLECTION

1. How did the tree in Nebuchadnezzar's dream represent him?

2. According to the angel, for what purpose was the tree cut down? For how long?

3. When he knew the dream's meaning, why was Daniel upset?

4. What was Nebuchadnezzar urged to do by Daniel to prevent the dream's fulfillment?

5. What were some of Nebuchadnezzar's accomplishments?

6. What did the king do to regain his sanity and his throne?

QUESTIONS FOR DISCUSSION

1. Have you ever noticed self-destructive pride in someone, but they were blind to it in themselves? Describe that occasion.

2. Do you consider "It's not bragging if it's true" to be a true or false statement? Why?

3. Why is it important to confess God as ruler of kings?

4. What are you often tempted to take credit for instead of giving glory to God?

5. Have you known someone who was genuinely happy in bitter circumstances? Describe their attitude. In your opinion, what made them so positive in the face of such negativity?

6. Have you known someone who was sour in spite of success? Describe their attitude. In your opinion, what made them so negative in spite of their positive circumstances?

7. How has God been merciful to you in spite of your pride?

6

WRITING ON THE WALL

DANIEL 5

Objective: To emphasize the certainty of God's judgment and the importance of turning to him in repentance before it is too late

INTRODUCTION

More than twenty years passed between Dan. 4-5. Nebuchadnezzar died in 562 B.C., and his son, Amel-Marduk, reigned for about two years. But he was assassinated in 560 by Neriglissar, whose brief reign of four years was very tumultuous. He was succeeded by his son, Labashi-Marduk, who held on to the throne for a remarkable nine months before being assassinated in a coup. This is how Nabonidus became king in 556. The events of Dan. 5 took place in October 539. As you can see, things unraveled very quickly for Babylon after Nebuchadnezzar's death.

Historical records confirm this chapter's account of Babylon's fall. As Isaiah had predicted many years before, Cyrus and his army overwhelmed the Babylonian Empire, and it passed into the pages of history with barely a whimper. Secular historians might claim that such happened because the Medo-Persian army under Cyrus' leadership was the superior force. But the Bible would have us confess that Babylon fell because she had been weighed in the scales of God's justice and had proven lacking.

Sin had reached its full measure. God had had enough.

EXAMINATION

Read Daniel 5:1-12. Years before, Jeremiah predicted that Babylon would collapse during a feast (51:39). Sure enough, Belshazzar held a feast for a large number of the aristocracy. When we first read this story, we are left with the impression that nothing was imminent—just a spoiled king having a party.

But Babylon knew it was about to be attacked (though not necessarily overrun) by Cyrus' army. This feast took place on the night of October 12, 539. Days earlier, two of Babylon's major cities had fallen, the main army had surrendered, and King Nabonidus had fled (he was later captured). Cyrus was now on his way to Babylon. Thus, Belshazzar had gathered the "Who's Who" of the city to invoke the protection of the gods so that mighty Babylon might not fall.

Part of the revelry included something Nebuchadnezzar had never done—the sacred vessels from the Jerusalem Temple were brought in so that the party guests could drink from them. By drinking from these vessels, perhaps Belshazzar and his nobles were reminding their gods of past victories and soliciting their protection now that Cyrus was at their back door. But what the king did was like spitting in God's eye. Though Belshazzar believed the vessels were proof of Yahweh's impotence, the exact opposite was true.

As the king and his friends exchanged toasts to the gods, a mysterious hand began to write words "on the plaster of the wall of the king's palace, opposite the lampstand" (v. 5). God's choice of a detached hand to deliver this message to Belshazzar is intriguing. In ancient times, casualty counts after a battle were often tabulated by collecting the severed right hands of those KIA. A lifeless, detached hand would then have symbolized a vanquished foe. But the hand that wrote these words did not belong to a defeated, dead god, but a living God of heaven, the very God Belshazzar believed he had defeated! Belshazzar's response is as comical as it is pathetic. The phrase "his limbs gave way" is literally "the knots of his loins were loosened (or untied)." To put it delicately, Belshazzar needed new underwear!

As his predecessor had done, Belshazzar summoned the wise men and offered a startling promotion to third in the kingdom (he couldn't offer #2—he was #2, and Daddy was #1), along with royal clothes and a gold chain. But just as Nebuchadnezzar had discovered, the wise men were impotent to explain the message. So in comes the queen. The queen mother was often a very powerful figure in the ancient Near East—so powerful on this occasion that she arrived uninvited (cf. Esth. 4:11) and ordered Belshazzar to summon Daniel.

Read Daniel 5:13-23. Upon Daniel's entrance, Belshazzar seemed skeptical of his aptitude. The king scornfully brought up the fact that Daniel was one of the exiles from Judah, as if this somehow equated the prophet to a country bumpkin and invalidated his many decades of loyal, competent service to the Empire. Nevertheless, the king acknowledged Daniel's reputation and offered the same reward to Daniel that had been extended to the wise men. But Daniel refused. What he was about to say would be difficult to swallow, and he wanted to avoid all appearances that he was in this for the money. Only after he gave the interpretation did Daniel accept the king's rewards, but Belshazzar might as well have offered Monopoly money.

Daniel reminded the bratty king that Nebuchadnezzar had embodied the totality of Babylon's splendor and enjoyed absolute power over the known world, but that "the Most High God" had given him this splendor and power (v. 18). When his pride had become too much, Nebuchadnezzar had been punished by God "until he knew that the Most High God rules the kingdom of mankind and sets over it whom he will" (v. 21). Though Belshazzar was acquainted with this well-known event, he had not taken it to heart. Instead, he had been foolish enough to lift himself up "against the Lord of heaven" (v. 23) and effectively spit in God's eye.

Read Daniel 5:24-31. In explaining the handwriting to the king, Daniel read the words as nouns (i.e. monetary weights) but interpreted them as verbs. This was the meaning of the inscription:

- *Mene, Mene*: As a noun, the term stood for a mina or denomination of money; as a verb, the word means "to number." It is mentioned twice since it has a double meaning—"to count" and "to fix the limit of." Because God is sovereign, knowing the end from the beginning (Isa. 46:10), he has fixed the days of every empire and ruler. No one reigns indefinitely.

- *Tekel*: Tekel or "shekel" was 1/60th of a mina; the verb form meant "to weigh." The moral state of Babylon had reached a level God would no longer tolerate. Their sins had reached their full measure. While God judges the individual in the hereafter, he judges nations in the here-and-now.

- *Parsin*: The noun referred to a half-shekel; the verb meant "to divide." God would prove his supremacy over Babylon by dividing it and giving it to Persia.

The king kept his word and clothed Daniel in purple, brought him jewelry, and proclaimed him third-most-powerful in the Empire. But the prophet knew the rewards were meaningless anyway—"that very night," the Medes and Persians captured Babylon.

The Greek historians Herodotus and Xenophon confirm the biblical record. Herodotus says Cyrus captured the city by redirecting the flow of the Euphrates, and his troops waded along the waterless riverbed where it passed under the city walls. Xenophon records how Cyrus' generals came upon Belshazzar with a dagger in hand, attempting suicide, but they "overpowered him" and executed him. They both note that these events took place on a night when seemingly all Babylon was having a party.

APPLICATION

Time Is Running Out. Belshazzar should have learned from the mistakes of Nebuchadnezzar, but he didn't. The Lord is patient with us, giving us many opportunities to turn to him to be saved from coming destruction (2 Pet. 3:9). It is a witness to his grace that he does not take our lives the first time we sin—that is surely what we deserve. On how many occasions have you intentionally disobeyed God, yet he did not strip you of life "that very night" as he did Belshazzar? Perhaps, in the back of your mind, you have been silencing the voice warning you of the need to be reconciled to God, but you ignore this voice, planning to make things right when it's more convenient. How many more chances will you receive before your sins reach their limit, your time runs out, and God has had enough? As Paul reminds us in Rom. 2:4, to delay our repentance is to scorn God's grace.

Missed Opportunities. Throughout the party, Belshazzar was drinking pretty heavily. With all the alcohol he consumed, I wonder if he ever knew what was going on? Had he not been drunk, might he have repented and averted disaster? One does not have to be literally intoxicated to miss the many opportunities God affords us to repent and return to him in submission and obedience. All that is required to "miss it" is a heart obsessed with temporary things on earth and not eternal ones in heaven (Col. 3:2-4). But the moment we awake from our drunken slumber—the moment we say "Yes!" to God and "No!" to the world—that's when true life begins! "Awake, O sleeper, and arise from the dead, and Christ will shine on you" (Eph. 5:14).

God's Certain Judgment. Reflecting on this chapter, James Montgomery Boice wrote, "The only thing more certain for us than death and taxes is the final judgment." For us, "the writing is on the wall," and it is not as mysterious or enigmatic as it was for Belshazzar. On the final day, God will judge all people according to their deeds (Rev. 20:13). And since we all have sinned, our doom is eternal punishment apart from God. But this is not the last word! In Christ, the written record against us is nullified (Col. 2:14)! In Christ, we don't stand condemned (Rom. 8:1)! God's wrath is a righteous, yet terrible thing. Don't wait a second longer, or it might be too late! Jesus is the only refuge from the wrath of God (Rom. 5:9). "Kiss the Son, lest he be angry, and you perish in the way, for his wrath is quickly kindled. Blessed are all who take refuge in him" (Psa. 2:12). Only in Jesus can you escape the certain and terrible judgment of a righteous God!

CONCLUSION

In his final moments, instead of turning to the true God for help, Belshazzar arrogantly appealed to his own false gods and spat in God's eye. In our own lives, we often show contempt for God's grace by not heeding his warning to repent before it is too late. We need Paul's reminder that today is the day of salvation (2 Cor. 6:2). Death or Christ could come at any moment. Though the text is silent on this issue, it is easy to believe that, had Belshazzar sincerely repented, Babylon's doom might have been averted as was Nineveh's during Jonah's day. But he didn't, and we will never know. But the New Testament assures us that, while life is still ours and breath is still in our lungs, God graciously welcomes all sinners back home.

QUESTIONS FOR REFLECTION

1. What had happened to the Babylonian Empire in the days leading up to Belshazzar's dinner party?

2. By drinking from the Temple vessels, what was Belshazzar attempting to do? What was he really doing?

3. Based on what we learned in Lesson #1, how were the captured Temple vessels symbols of God's power, not weakness?

4. What did the detached hand represent in ancient times?

5. Why could Belshazzar not offer Daniel #2 in the kingdom?

LESSON 6: WRITING ON THE WALL

6. Why did Daniel initially reject Belshazzar's reward?

7. According to Daniel, what did the inscription mean?

QUESTIONS FOR DISCUSSION

1. According to Daniel, what was Belshazzar's sin?

2. Though his sin was similar, why was Belshazzar (unlike Nebuchadnezzar) not given an opportunity to repent?

3. Though it is unpleasant to think about, why is it important to emphasize the certainty of God's judgment against sin?

4. How is failing to take seriously God's judgment actually a way of showing scorn and disdain for his grace?

5. Why do so many people delay in taking their sins seriously?

6. Have you been guilty of not taking sin seriously? How so?

7

THE LIONS' DEN

DANIEL 6

Objective: To explore the importance of integrity and faithfulness in prayer in the lives of God's people

INTRODUCTION

Daniel and lions go together like peanut butter and jelly. When you think of the biblical Daniel, this story comes to mind. It's what kids immediately associate with Daniel, in part because of cuddly stuffed lions in Sunday school and the fun song that goes, "Daniel, Daniel, Daniel, Daniel, Daniel in the li- li- lions' … den." But have we robbed this story of its horror and ferocity by making it into such a lovable children's tale? To contemplate a night in a den of lions, imagine the first time you saw the movie *Jaws* or *Jurassic Park*. But instead of fancy film work or CGI, these were real lions!

In the case of many martyrs throughout church history, God in his wisdom chose not to deliver his saints from suffering. As was the case with the Fiery Furnace scene, these stories are not intended to give us the false hope that God will deliver us from every trial, but that he is present with us in our suffering, and that nothing can separate us from his love. The apostle Paul knew God had preserved his life on countless occasions because Paul's ministry wasn't yet complete. But there came a day when Rome's executioner laid the axe on the apostle's neck. Only then did God bring him "safely into his heavenly kingdom" (2 Tim. 4:18).

In the case of the Fiery Furnace, Daniel's three friends refused to worship idols, even if it meant death. Theirs was a refusal to do something they knew was wrong. Here, Daniel refused to cease doing something he knew to be right, even if it meant death. The call to faithfulness demands we say No! to some things while maintaining an eager Yes! to others. Through it all, we are confident God is with us until he brings us safely into his heavenly kingdom.

EXAMINATION

Read Daniel 6:1-9. The Medo-Persian Empire stretched from India to Ethiopia and was composed of 120 satrapies in Daniel's day—satrap meant "protector of the empire." Over these 120 satraps were three "administrators" or "commissioners." Part of Daniel's responsibilities as one of the commissioners was to prevent military revolts and oversee the collection of tax revenue for the king to ensure that he was not cheated. This obviously was a position reserved for only those men with the highest integrity. Daniel even began to distinguish himself over the other two administrators to the point that "the king planned to set him over the whole kingdom" (v. 3).

Out of envy, the other two administrators and several of the satraps plotted to ruin Daniel. They sought for cause (e.g. dishonest with money, a trouble-maker) to have him dismissed or worse, but their search was fruitless. Daniel "was faithful, and no error or fault was found in him" (v. 4). Daniel was so filled with integrity that the only way to get rid of him was to pit his allegiance to God vs. his allegiance to king and country. So they made a proposal to Darius that no one be allowed to pray for a month to any man or god except Darius.

Punishment was being cast into the lions' den. The word translated "den" simply means "pit," so the lions' den in this story was likely a large, underground space similar to a cave with a hole at the top (to feed the lions) that could be sealed with a stone. The entire plot hinged on two things: Daniel's faithfulness to his God and the well-attested irrevocability of "the law of the Medes and the Persians" (vv. 8, 12, 15).

Read Daniel 6:10-18. Once the decree had been made, Daniel had several options. He could have simply abstained from praying for a month. He could have found a place to pray more private than his upper room (i.e. a room on his flat roof with latticed windows). But Daniel refused to "scale back" what he was publicly known to do. He could not in good conscience alter his practice.

Daniel's enemies were waiting on him to violate the law, and they did not have to wait long. They quickly informed the king of Daniel's disobedience, painting him as one all too eager to scorn the king and the decree. They insinuated to Darius that Daniel's insubordinate act made him a dangerous subversive. But Darius obviously knew better than to buy into this notion that Daniel was a rebel. The king "was much distressed" when he heard this and spent the rest of the day seeking a way out of the dilemma. In this scene, Darius is to be pitied. It is an ironic shame that so powerful a king as Darius could not bring about the one thing he wanted to happen!

Before the opening to the den was sealed, Darius encouraged Daniel: "May your God, whom you serve continually, deliver you!" (v. 16). So great had Daniel's witness been in the court of the king that Darius believed it possible his favorite employee would indeed survive the night by the power of God. Then the opening to the den was closed with a stone, and both the king and Daniel's enemies sealed it with their signet rings.

Read Daniel 6:19-28. A new day had scarcely dawned when Darius beat a path back to the lions' den, desperate to know whether Daniel had been delivered from danger (v. 20). To the king's inquiry, Daniel replied that God had indeed delivered him. An angel had been sent to shut the lions' mouths (Heb. 11:33). When Daniel was lifted out of the den, it was discovered that he was completely unharmed because he had trusted in God (v. 23). Once out of the den, Darius threw Daniel's conspirators and their families to the lions. In the ancient Near East, anyone bringing a false charge against someone was punished in like manner (cf. Deut. 19:16-21; Esth. 7:10), and their families often with them (cf. Josh. 7:24-26; Esth. 9:24-25)

As Nebuchadnezzar had done previously, Darius sent a letter—a new decree—to the nations. Many of the theological themes of the book of Daniel are echoed here: God is eternal, as is his kingdom, and he has the absolute power to save and work miracles at will.

APPLICATION

Integrity Under Fire. The reader has to admit that the plot of Daniel's enemies was perfectly schemed. It rested partly on the ego of an emperor, but also on Daniel's unwavering commitment to his God. When they first began to plot against Daniel, they naturally looked for a flaw in his character. As one of the top three administrators in the Empire, Daniel would have not lacked for opportunities for corruption. But he was squeaky clean, and his enemies knew it. Their admission in v. 5, that they would have to use Daniel's faith against him, is revealing of Daniel's character. God's people today must live lives of high integrity so that we give no opportunity to the wicked to disparage us or our Lord (cf. 1 Pet. 2:12).

Faithfulness in Prayer. Daniel preferred to face the lions than go a month without praying. When he received word that the decree was now law, he proceeded undeterred to pray anyway. Daniel considered fellowship with God to be more precious than his personal, bodily safety. Can the same be said for us? When Christ was on earth, he lived and ministered among Jews who were very accustomed to praying. Yet, our Lord's disciples saw in his prayer life a depth that they did not possess. Hence, the request, "Lord, teach us to pray" (Luke 11:1). If we can learn to be faithful and persistent in prayer, considering it a great privilege and rich blessing, rather than a spiritual chore or superficial mark of maturity, then we will be able to withstand the storms of life as Daniel did until Jesus calls us home.

Keep Calm & Keep On. It's a shame that Christians seem to only get up in arms about doing what's right when that action is threatened. We only speak out against gay marriage when it's legalized; we only speak out against abortion when Planned Parenthood pushes the envelope. Notice, however, that when Daniel heard the decree prohibiting prayer for a month, he simply kept doing what was already his custom. It is hypocrisy to start a habit indignantly because that action has been banned or discouraged. Such an attitude smacks too much of brash pride or hubris than sincere faithfulness. Let us be doing things now that we know we should do, rather than delaying until seasons of persecution.

CONCLUSION

God has not promised to deliver us safely from every threat. What he has promised, however, is to be present with us in every trial. Fellowship with God's presence is a very precious thing, and Daniel was willing to face any punishment if it meant uninterrupted fellowship with his God. When we face trials in life, let us treasure God's presence with us above all else. Let us, like Daniel, be people of high moral integrity and uncompromising faith, regardless of the cost. And, like Daniel, let us continue to do the things we know God expects of us, confident that the Lord is always in control.

QUESTIONS FOR REFLECTION

1. Is this story a promise that God will deliver his people from every threat? Why/why not?

2. What did Daniel's enemies do when they found no flaw in his character?

3. What was Daniel's response when he heard of the decree?

4. As Darius is forced to leave Daniel in the lions' den overnight, how does the narrator portray the king as a pitiful figure?

5. Why were the families of Daniel's enemies also thrown into the den along with the perpetrators?

QUESTIONS FOR DISCUSSION

1. In your personal experience, have you allowed this story's "kid-friendly factor" to keep you from appreciating the horrible nature of this story? How so?

2. When he heard the decree, did Daniel continue a long-standing habit or begin a new one? Why is this important?

3. If this story does not teach that God always rescues his people from trials, what does it teach?

4. Why is God's presence in the den of despair more precious than deliverance from every earthly trial?

5. How can Christians develop Daniel's integrity?

6. How can the church help Christians foster Daniel's prayer habits?

8

THE FOUR BEASTS
DANIEL 7

Objective: To celebrate the supremacy of Christ, God's love for his people, and the Lord's sovereignty over every evil power

INTRODUCTION

When I first decided to write a book on Daniel, I knew I would no longer be able to avoid the second half of Daniel. Beginning with Dan. 7, the stoic, levelheaded Daniel we have come to know in chapters 1-6 gives way to a strange, unpredictable, borderline psychotic Daniel in chapters 7-12. There are visions and dreams and scary creatures—Oh my! To complicate matters, there are a lot of strong opinions on the latter half of Daniel. Scholars say one thing; televangelists claim another. Do these visions concern events that have already taken place? Or are they a roadmap to the end of time? How are we to know?

In his commentary, scholar Tremper Longman III claims that this second half of Daniel remains "one of the most enigmatic sections of the Old Testament." These are important chapters, but the odds are against our understanding them correctly and completely. But their difficulty should not scare us away. Instead, these chapters will give us a grand view of God, calling us to worship and to realign our priorities, as well as filling our hearts with joyful expectation.

EXAMINATION

Read Daniel 7:1-14. This vision is dated to Belshazzar's first year (c. 550-549 B.C.), meaning the events of Dan. 5 were a mere ten years in the future. In 550, Cyrus usurped the throne from Astyages the Mede and forged a new empire; though few realized it at the time, the political landscape of the ancient world was headed for violent change. This vision gave Daniel notice of what was to come.

The "great sea" (v. 2) could refer to the Mediterranean, but given the passage's apocalyptic nature, "great sea" likely means the cosmic sea that symbolized chaos (cf. Gen. 1:2; Rev. 13:1; 17:15). The "four winds of heaven" represent God's ability to exert his will on people and nations (cf. Zech. 2:6; Rev. 7:1).

Daniel saw four beasts emerge from the sea, and these beasts represented four empires. The text is clear that these are not natural animals, but mutant hybrids, meaning they represent a perversion of God's will, though they remain under God's control.

The first beast, a lion with eagle's wings, represented the Babylonian Empire. Archaeologists have found numerous winged lions among the ruins of Babylon, and the Bible compares Babylon/Nebuchadnezzar with a lion and an eagle on several occasions (e.g. Jer. 4:7-8; Lam. 4:19; Ezek. 17:3, 12). The beast's feathers are plucked, marking "a loss of ferocity and power, which was most certainly the case in the last decades of the once all-conquering Babylonian regime."

The second beast, a bear, is assumed to represent the Medo/Persian Empire that replaced Babylon. The bear gnawing on three bones

may relate to Cyrus conquering three kingdoms to forge his empire before moving on to Babylon and Egypt.

The third beast, a leopard with four wings and heads, symbolized Alexander the Great's speedy conquest of the known world. He forged an empire, only for it to be divided among four generals after Alexander died at the young age of 33.

The fourth beast was far worse than the others. Daniel emphatically describes it as "terrifying and dreadful and exceedingly strong." Its iron teeth, its ten horns, and an eleventh, smaller horn all conjure within the reader a strong sense of terror and revulsion.

But before we can linger on the hideous nature of the fourth beast, the scene quickly shifts to a throne room in heaven. Everything has changed. Where there had formerly been chaos, hostility, and oppression, there is now goodness and justice and order. The Ancient of Days is depicted as righteous, holy, and pure. Before God, the wickedness of the fourth beast is recounted, and Daniel then witnesses the beast judged, sentenced, and destroyed. The three other beasts were stripped of their power, but their lives were prolonged.

Then came One "like the Son of Man" (i.e. One who looked like a man, rather than a beast). Unlike the dominion of the four beasts, the Son of Man was given a kingdom that would never pass away. This figure can be none other than Jesus, who spoke of riding on the clouds of heaven (Matt. 24:30; 26:64).

Read Daniel 7:15-28. Daniel remained troubled, so an angel explained to him the meaning of the vision. The four beasts represented four kings or empires. The terrifying nature of the fourth beast is again emphasized. Specifically, the little horn of this fourth beast would make "war with the saints and [prevail] over them." But God would judge the little horn and destroy it, along with the fourth beast.

Note that the Lord would allow the fourth beast to torment his people "for a time, times, and half a time" (v. 25), a phrase meaning 3½ or half of 7, a number of perfection. Put another way, a full season of punishment is often expressed as "seven times" (cf. 4:16, 32), so 3½ times means God sometimes shortens the season of trial allotted to his people (cf. Rev. 11:2-3; 12:6, 14; 13:4-5). Note also that the little horn's evil was not fully revealed until after it had been judged and destroyed by a righteous Ancient of Days and a victorious Son of Man. This chapter may not give us a detailed roadmap for the future, but its symbolism does affirm the final result of history: God wins, Jesus reigns, and the saints inherit an eternal kingdom.

APPLICATION

The Corruption of Power. God ordained civil government, has called Christians to submit to it (Rom. 13:1), and wants us to pray for it (1 Tim. 2:1-2). But this does not mean God approves of everything governments do. The mutant nature of the four beasts reminds us that every government eventually becomes intoxicated with its own power and perverts God's will. Even a democracy collapses into chaos if its citizens are immoral. Thus, God's people should not place too much trust in any form of government (cf. Jer. 17:5). Rather, our affection, passion, hope, and trust should all be in God, the Ancient of Days, who reigns over all in justice, holiness, and sovereignty.

The Church Under Fire. Daniel was horrified to see the fourth beast and the eleventh horn wreak so much havoc on God's people. Indeed, God's people would be given over to the eleventh horn "for a time, times, and half a time." But though persecution is our lot on earth (2 Tim. 3:12), it will not last forever. God eventually judges and punishes tormentors of his church, so our hope is in the return of the Son of Man. On that day, he will inherit a kingdom that will never pass away, and vindication and eternal joy will be our reward. Every tyrant and beast will bow his knee before Christ. Thus, the church must not become intoxicated by worldly power or immobilized by fear. Let us act decisively, speak courageously, and love passionately.

The Beast Forgiven. It's human nature to blame others for all that's wrong in the world (e.g. Republicans blame big government, and Democrats blame big business). But the Bible is clear that "the beast" lives in all of us. In Romans, Paul declares both Jews and Gentiles to be guilty of immorality (1:18-3:20)—all have sinned (3:23). But later on, the apostle imagines another courtroom scene (8:33-34). Citizens of the kingdom of the Son of Man are no longer under condemnation (8:1). Instead of punishment, we are justified and exonerated. Against any angel, ruler, evil power, "we are more than conquerors through him who loved us" (8:37)! Though the beast lives in each of us, God—in Christ—proved to us the depths of his love.

DIGGING DEEPER

A small (yet important) genre of literature in Scripture is apocalyptic literature. It was very familiar to Jews and Christians c. 200 BC-AD 200, but it's not so familiar to Christians today. Apocalyptic literature is featured prominently in Dan. 7-12, Revelation, and parts of Isaiah, Ezekiel, and Zechariah, as well as Jewish literature from the intertestamental period. In light of its difficult nature, here are a few important rules for interpreting apocalyptic literature.

Don't force literalness. Apocalyptic literature is most abused when well-meaning Bible students force a literal interpretation on the text. This is not always God's intent (cf. Num. 12:6-8). Very seldom does this literature mean exactly what it says—e.g. "seventy" doesn't always mean the number between 69 and 71!

Don't be dogmatic. Books like Daniel and Revelation must be read and interpreted with a healthy dose of humility. At times, these passages will seem like a Rubik's cube, the sides of which were never color-matched to begin with. If Daniel, who was famous for his wisdom, couldn't completely understand these visions, we won't either. Let's be humble about what we cannot prove.

Don't miss the forest for the trees. We can't become so bogged down in decoding every symbol that we miss the ultimate message. If some of the details of Dan. 7-12 remain confusing, its main point is not.

CONCLUSION

Throughout the 19th century, many believed that the human condition was improving. But the 20th century proved to be among the bloodiest in history, proving that for all our technological advancement, we're still plagued by sin and corruption on a fundamental level. Christians should care about injustice and suffering in the world, but we also should realize that things will not be made right completely until the Son of Man returns in the clouds. And as long as the Ancient of Days remains seated on heaven's throne, the people of God have no reason to fear the future.

QUESTIONS FOR REFLECTION

1. What do the sea and the four winds of heaven represent?

2. What significance is there in the fact that these beasts are mutant hybrids and not natural animals?

3. How does Daniel describe the fourth beast?

4. How is the Ancient of Days depicted as righteous, holy, and pure? How is the totality of his judgment represented?

5. What does "a time, times, and half a time" mean?

6. What was Daniel's response to this vision?

QUESTIONS FOR DISCUSSION

1. Though God ordained civil governments, they often act against his will. How can governments pervert God's will?

2. How is the church a fundamental threat to worldly power?

3. What hope does this passage give the suffering Christian?

4. Why is it important to confess "the beast is in all of us"?

5. Though some of its details might be confusing, what would you say is the main point of this vision in Dan. 7?

9

THE RAM & THE GOAT

DANIEL 8

Objective: To affirm that persecution always has a purpose, but that God is in complete control of the oppression and the oppressor

INTRODUCTION

In the movie *Bruce Almighty*, a news reporter is suddenly given power by the Almighty to exercise divine prerogative and right a few wrongs. Along with the miraculous ability to part his tomato soup as if it were the Red Sea and transform his clunker into a sleek sports car, Bruce also had to answer prayers. The prayers became so voluminous that he eventually began affirming all the requests automatically. But in the film, God's (played by Morgan Freeman) response to such a strategy is a stinging indictment of human nature: "Since when do people have a clue what they want?"

It requires faith to see things from God's perspective, but when we do, we quickly realize how the wrong things attract us and the right things seem abominable. We blame God in bad situations, but we credit karma or count our lucky stars when things are good. How could we have a clue about what we really want—much less need?

Daniel 8 is a remarkable chapter because it contains a detailed prophecy about the fate of the Jews stretching 400 years beyond Daniel's life. The promises God made in this chapter came to pass, arguably down to the very day. In fact, the predictions in this chapter are so accurate that some scholars allege that they were made after the fact, but only because they are prejudiced against the miraculous!

However, the prophecies in this chapter were given, not to give the Jews a roadmap for the future, but to encourage them to trust God in dark times. If the Lord knew the future so intimately and exactly, "declaring the end from the beginning" (Isa. 46:10), then surely he could be trusted to work events to Israel's good and his glory. Left to ourselves, we wouldn't want to endure years of harsh persecution, but since when do people have a clue what they want? There is always a purpose when God's people are persecuted.

EXAMINATION

Read Daniel 8:1-14. This vision took place in Belshazzar's third year (548-547 BC). Daniel found himself on the banks of the Ulai canal in Susa, a fortress-city about 200 miles east of Babylon. At the time of this vision, it was the capital of Elam. Unlike Dan. 7, which was a dream, this was a vision during which Daniel was awake and conscious.

In the vision, he saw on the canal's bank a ram with one horn higher than the other (a very unusual detail). It charged to the west, north, and south and proved invincible. "He did as he pleased and became great" (v. 4). The ram signified the Medo-Persian Empire—Persian kings sported a golden ram's head on their helmets whenever they led their armies into battle. The lesser horn was Media, a nation that was initially great, but conquered by the Persians in 550 B.C., at which point Cyrus fused the two kingdoms together—"the higher [horn] came up last" (v. 3). From that point, Persia conquered nations to the west (Babylon, Syria, Lydia), north (Armenia, Scythia), and south (Egypt and Ethiopia). The Persian kingdom lasted more than 200 years and indeed "became great"—it amassed more territory than any empire before it.

Then a male goat appeared, charging furiously from the west with such speed that it didn't touch the ground. Two things stood out to Daniel: the goat's "conspicuous" horn and the goat's attitude. "In his powerful wrath," the goat charged at the ram with rage, broke the ram's two horns, then trampled and vanquished him. The goat, in turn, "became exceedingly great" (v. 8), meaning it was presumptuous or arrogant. But then its horn was broken and four more "conspicu-

ous horns" rose up in its place "toward the four winds of heaven."

The goat was the Greek Empire (the goat was an ancient symbol for Macedonia), and the first great horn was "the first king," known to us as Alexander the Great. Born in 356, Alexander assumed his father's throne at age 20 when Philip II was assassinated. The goat's wrath and rage had caught Daniel's attention, and for good reason. "Enraged" (8:7) means "to be embittered" or "maddened." Persia tried unsuccessfully to conquer Greece, but only succeeded in angering them. The campaigns of Darius I in 490 BC and of Xerxes a decade later had especially left many Greeks outraged, and Alexander exploited the memory of those events to inflame his troops. Within three short years, his army devastated Persian forces at the decisive battles of Granicus, Issus, and Arbela. Alexander "became exceedingly great" by conquering more territory than Persia had done, a total of some 1.5 million square miles stretching from Greece to India.

Then in Daniel's vision, "a little horn" also rose up and became "exceedingly great," particularly toward the south, east, and "the glorious land" (i.e. Palestine). The rise of the little horn reached "the host of heaven," and it trampled some of the host and stars of heaven (i.e. the Jews). The little horn became "as great as the Prince of the host" to the point that the regular burnt offering was stripped away and the sanctuary overthrown. Some of the host and the Temple services would be given to it; the little horn would "throw truth to the ground, and it will act and prosper."

At that point in the vision, two angels began conversing. One asked the other how long these things (i.e. the suffering of God's people) would last. This a significant question because it meant God's people would not be oppressed by this little horn forever. There is always an end to suffering, and it always comes in God's good timing. How long would the little horn be allowed to oppress God's people? The reply given to Daniel was "2,300 evenings and mornings," at which point the sanctuary would be restored. What are we to make of such a phrase, and of a little horn licensed with so much power?

Read Daniel 8:15-27. Having witnessed the vision, Daniel then saw a man (likely God) "between the banks of the Ulai," meaning he was hovering over the water. The "man" commanded Gabriel to explain the vision. The vision was "for the time of the end," meaning it concerned things that would happen at the end of a period of time, not the end of the world. Later, Gabriel said the vision concerned "the latter end of the indignation … the appointed time of the end" (v. 19), meaning God had appointed a period of time in which he would punish his people for their sins, but he had also ordained an end for this terrible string of events. In other words, "the end" of v. 17 points back to the question of v. 13—"For how long?" This vision is not about the end of the world; this is a very important distinction.

Just as Gabriel said, four separate kingdoms arose from Alexander's empire, but they did not have his power. When Alexander died, his kingdom was eventually divided among four of his generals, often known as the "Diadochi" (Greek for "successors"). Greece went to Cassander, Asia Minor to Lysimachus, Syria to Seleucus, and Egypt to Ptolemy.

Toward the end of the Greek Empire, one particular king (the little horn) with a "bold face" and the ability to understand "riddles" ascended the throne. This little horn is none other than the Seleucid king Antiochus IV. Consider that:

This king would come to power "at the latter end of the indignation" and "when the transgressors have reached their limit" (vv. 19, 23). "Indignation" here means God's wrath against his unfaithful people (cf. Isa. 10:5; Lam. 2:6). In the years leading up to Antiochus' reign, unfaithful Jews introduced the more pagan aspects of Greek culture into the practice of Judaism. The book of 1 Maccabees says these Jews built a gymnasium in Jerusalem to exercise in the nude, they had surgery to reverse their circumcision, practiced idolatry, and profaned the Sabbath. Because of their transgressions, God would bring his indignation against Israel once again in the form of Antiochus' tyranny.

This king would have a "bold face," meaning he would be hard, determined, and unyielding. He would be "one who understands riddles," meaning he was politically savvy and skilled at flattery. This fits the general portrait of Antiochus as presented by historians.

This king would have tremendous power, "but not by his own power." In other words, his power would not be earned, but be given to him by a superior. Antiochus gained his authority through less-than-noble means. His brother, Seleucus IV, was assassinated, and Antiochus assumed the throne only after incarcerating Seleucus' son, Demetrius, in Rome. During his reign, Antiochus enjoyed successful military exploits against Egypt ("toward the south," v. 9), Babylon, Persia ("the east"), and Palestine ("the glorious land").

This king would "cause fearful destruction." He would be successful in destroying "mighty men" and "the saints," and in making "deceit prosper" while he reigned. On one occasion, Antiochus launched a surprise attack against Jerusalem after assuring them he wanted peace. On another, he massacred several Jews on the Sabbath, knowing they would not defend themselves on a day of rest.

This king would elevate himself against God, "the Prince of princes." Also, "In his own mind he shall become great" (v. 25). Antiochus assumed the title *Theou Epiphanes*, meaning "God revealed," but his critics changed it to *Epimanes*, meaning "madman." Antiochus "threw truth to the ground" by ordering Torah scrolls to be burned. The first king mentioned in the book of Daniel, Jehoiakim, discovered bad things happen to those who burn the Word of God (Jer. 36:20-31); Antiochus would fare no better.

Eventually, the little horn would be broken, "but by no human hand." Just as God had given Antiochus his power (via Satan), God took it away. The Jewish historian Josephus relates how Antiochus besieged the Persian city of Elymais, but was rebuffed and had to flee to Babylon with a decimated army. At Babylon, he heard of how his forces in Judea had been defeated by the Maccabees. With his world crashing down around him, Antiochus "fell into a distemper." While on his deathbed, he confessed to his friends "that this calamity was sent upon him for the miseries he had brought upon the Jewish nation, while he plundered their temple and condemned their God," (*Antiquities* 12.9.1).

Daniel's response to the vision was severe. It left him physically sick for several days, and even when he returned to work, he remained "appalled by the vision and did not understand it" (cf. 7:28). In our quest to fully understand Daniel's enigmatic visions, we must remind ourselves regularly that not even Daniel understood them perfectly. We can take our best shots, but we can't be dogmatic that our interpretation is the correct one. Even the prophets wrote sometimes of things they did not fully understand (1 Pet. 1:10-12). The best we can do with difficult passages is to "pay attention" to "the prophetic word … as to a lamp shining in a dark place, until the day dawns and the morning star rises in your hearts" (2 Pet. 1:19).

APPLICATION

Purifying Persecution. God allowed Antiochus to persecute Israel in order to purify them. Persecution is God's cleansing agent; Antiochus did not rise to power until "the transgressors [had] reached their limit" (v. 23). The church must realize that any persecution we endure might be intended by God as discipline to purify and sanctify us—a realignment of our priorities (cf. Heb. 12:5-11). But it is also true that the tyrant who oppresses us will also suffer God's wrath. God is sovereign over the oppression and the oppressor.

God Remains Sovereign. God rules over history's "movers and shakers." Alexander deservedly garnered the moniker "the Great," but Dan. 8 perfectly illustrates how he was only a pawn on God's chessboard. So too was Antiochus. The first part of v. 12 contains a passive verb, "will be given over," which is another way of stating that God permitted Antiochus' reign of terror just as he had allowed Pharaoh's stubborn heart and Satan's oppression of Job. No one, not even the Prince of Darkness, can do anything without God's permission.

Trust & Obey. One does not have to understand all of Dan. 8 to appreciate the necessity of faith in the midst of confusing and trying times. If a period of oppression should come upon the church, how will we respond? The only proper response is trust. Trust that God knows the end from the beginning, that he loves his people unconditionally, and that he is always faithful to do what is best for us. And to our trust, let us add obedience… "For there is no other way to be happy in Jesus, but to trust and obey."

CONCLUSION

Left to ourselves, we wouldn't want to endure years of harsh persecution, but since when do people have a clue what they want? If God could use Paul's imprisonment to further the gospel (Phil. 1:12-14); if God could use the worst day in history, a day now known as "Good Friday," to bless his people, then nothing is out of his control. This chapter gives us the assurance that God knows the future, that he is Lord of all, and that it is up to us to trust him in all things, for thereby we overcome the world (1 John 5:4).

QUESTIONS FOR REFLECTION

1. What two empires did the ram and goat represent?

2. What two things stood out to Daniel about the goat?

3. Describe the actions of the little horn in the vision.

4. What historical figure can be identified with the little horn?

5. List other biblical examples of God's control of wicked rulers.

6. Describe Daniel's response to this vision.

7. Do you believe suffering always has a purpose?

QUESTIONS FOR DISCUSSION

1. How can persecution be a blessing for God's people?

2. How can we discern the purpose of persecution?

3. What comfort or pain is there in the fact that God remains sovereign over the most oppressive of all world rulers?

4. Read Psa. 2:10-12. What connection does this passage have with Dan. 8?

5. In your opinion, why did God choose to give Daniel a preview of the next 400 years of Jewish history?

10

THE SEVENTY WEEKS

DANIEL 9

Objective: To emphasize the horrible nature of sin and to praise God for his plan to redeem us from it

INTRODUCTION

In 1987, Edgar C. Whisenant became famous for a short book titled *88 Reasons Why the Rapture Could Be in 1988*. Of course, the Rapture didn't happen in 1988, but this is one of many predictions made by Mr. Whisenant that never came true. The reason I mention this book is because much of Whisenant's reasoning was based in part on his understanding of the seventy weeks in Dan. 9.

Another failed end-times prognosticator, Harold Camping, published a book in 1992 alleging that 1994 would bring with it the end of all things. He too was wrong. But that didn't stop him from readjusting his prognostication and then saying that the end would come in 2011. Again, it didn't, and as you may have already suspected, much of Mr. Camping's reasoning came from his (mis) interpretation of the seventy weeks. In fact, the Second Coming has been predicted over 200 times since World War II alone, and many of those predictions have utilized Daniel's seventy weeks as part of their justification. Ironically, Jewish rabbis in the Talmud cursed those who used Dan. 9 to calculate the end of time!

This chapter is notoriously difficult to interpret. Jack Lewis says, "Few biblical passages have been the subject of more speculation than has this one." But this does not mean the chapter is irrelevant. For all of its confusion, Dan. 9 is about our need to glorify Christ for what he did in destroying the power of sin and Satan at the cross; it is about our greatest problem, sin, and how God planned to orchestrate our rescue.

EXAMINATION

Read Daniel 9:1-19. During Cyrus' [i.e. Darius'] first year as king (539 B.C.), Daniel decided to study the book of Jeremiah, particularly chapters 25 and 29. These passages predicted the Jews would be exiled for seventy years. Now that there had been a regime change from Babylon to Persia, would the exile end and Daniel's people be allowed to return home?

Daniel's prayer was accompanied by fasting and customary grief practices such as donning sackcloth and sitting in ashes. The prophet began by praising God's greatness and covenant faithfulness in spite of Israel having been unfaithful with her sin and rebellion. In times of uncertainty, there is arguably no greater confession we can make than the fact that God is great and faithful to his people.

God's people have no entitlement to his compassion or faithfulness. Like ancient Israel, we have not always been obedient to the Lord, so he owes us nothing. Daniel acknowledged that Israel had gotten just what they deserved in being exiled from their home. Daniel poured out his pain over how Israel bore tremendous embarrassment and shame for her treatment of Yahweh. At any moment, the damage could have been mitigated had Israel repented and "entreated the favor of the LORD" (v. 13), but they never did.

It is then that Daniel begged the Lord to relent in punishment and no longer be angry. Jerusalem and Israel had become "a byword"—objects of ridicule among the other nations. On the heels of the covenant curses spoken by Moses in Deut. 28 had come the promise of restoration (Deut. 30:2-3), and Daniel appealed to this promise in his prayer to God. But ridicule of Israel and faithfulness to his own promise were just two parts of God's overall motive to relent and restore his people. His one singular motive was his own glory. God always acts in order to glorify himself.

Read Daniel 9:20-27. While Daniel was still praying, Gabriel came to him and announced that "seventy weeks" were required to accomplish six goals related to the Jews and Jerusalem (that last part is an important detail). Are these seventy literal weeks? Most interpreters consider the phrase to mean 490 years (i.e. seventy sevens). But how are we to know that we should read "weeks" as "years"?

We'll come back to the 70 weeks vs. 490 years question. For now, notice the goals of these "seventy sevens" according to Gabriel:

1. "to finish the transgression"
2. "to put an end to sin"
3. "to atone for iniquity"
4. "to bring in everlasting righteousness"
5. "to seal both vision and prophet"
6. "to anoint a most holy place."

Gabriel divided the seventy weeks into three periods:

7 weeks: extending "from the going out of the word to restore and build Jerusalem to the coming of an anointed one, a prince."

62 weeks: this period included the rebuilding of Jerusalem, complete with "squares and moat," meaning it would be a complete, legitimate city once again.

A final week: during this period, an anointed one would be cut off and have nothing. Jerusalem would be destroyed, and the destroyer would then be destroyed.

At this, Gabriel assumedly disappears and we are left with a lot of unanswered questions.

- What does "the going out of the word" refer to?
- Who is the "anointed one"? Are there two anointed ones in mind instead of one?
- Who are the people that destroy Jerusalem and the Temple?
- Are the "seventy weeks" contiguous or are there "prophetic gaps" in between?
- What was the "strong covenant" and "wing of abominations"?

By now, you can see why this chapter has been so confusing. Smarter people than I have wrestled with this passage, only to come up empty on an interpretation that satisfies everyone, so I'm not about to pretend I have all the answers. However, there are certain details that point us to the big picture.

We should be cautious about forcing a literal interpretation on the "seventy weeks." Regardless of the date you pick to begin the seventy weeks, none terminates at both a conclusive and meaningful date. It's beyond me as to why some symbolically interpret "seventy weeks" as 490 years, but then become dogmatic about it being 490 literal years, rather than appreciating the phrase's symbolic meaning.

Moses warned that Israel would be punished "sevenfold" for her sins (Lev. 26:21), so we might be meant to interpret the seventy years of exile symbolically, namely as the perfect work of God to punish and restore his people. In the same way, seventy sevens (i.e. 70 x 7) represents God's "perfect upon perfect" timing to bring Jesus into the world. For all the murky confusion surrounding the "seventy weeks," the New Testament is clear its fulfillment is found in Christ.

- Jesus "finished the transgression" and "put an end to sin" (Rom. 5:6-10; Heb. 9:26).

- He atoned for iniquity (Heb. 7:23-8:6; 10:1-14) by offering himself up as a propitiation for our sins.

- He thereby ushered in "everlasting righteousness" (1 Cor. 1:30; 2 Cor. 5:21).

- Jesus sealed (i.e. was the fulfillment of) Old Testament prophecy (2 Cor. 1:20; Heb. 1:1-2; 1 Pet. 1:10-12).

- By his death and resurrection, Jesus annointed a new "most holy place" in our hearts (1 Cor. 6:19).

The final two verses of Dan. 9 allude to the destruction of Jerusalem and the Temple, which occurred in A.D. 70 at the hands of the Romans. Jesus himself had foreseen this terrible event and declared it to be God's punishment of Israel for having rejected Jesus as the Messiah (Luke 19:41-44). On another occasion, our Lord recalled "the abomination of desolation spoken of by the prophet Daniel" (Matt. 24:15) and warned his followers in Judea to "flee to the mountains" that they might be spared.

To summarize a very complicated lesson, I believe the "seventy weeks" are not to be interpreted literally as 490 years or any other chronological number, but symbolically as God's "fullness of time" in which he brought Christ into the world (cf. Gal. 4:4). Put another way, all six goals of the seventy weeks were fulfilled in Christ.

APPLICATION

The Gravity of Sin. In many church bulletins, the list of those with physical ailments outnumber those with spiritual needs (the names of those with cancer alone often take up half the page). We should certainly care about the physically sick and pray for them. But we must also confess with Daniel that God's people have a sin problem, and that we are in need of God's great mercy. Our sins should grieve us deeply, our terminology should reflect their hideous nature, and whenever we are forced to say them, these words should leave behind a very bitter taste. In his response to Daniel's prayer, God was more concerned with assuring Daniel that he would act against sin than he was giving Daniel a precise timetable of future events. As reflected in Daniel's prayer and Gabriel's message, God is most concerned with bringing himself glory, and only when God's people are heartbroken over sin can they properly glorify the Lord.

> When our Lord ascended into heaven and the Holy Spirit descended, there remained not one of the six items of Daniel 9:24 that was not fully accomplished.
>
> **PHILIP MAURO**

Praying for God's People. Our hearts warm at the thought of Daniel praying, not only for his contemporaries, but also for all the people of God who followed him. Visions of events that would take place centuries after Daniel's lifetime caused the old prophet to pray fervently for future citizens of God's kingdom. The church today has the same obligation to pray for all saints everywhere and in every time. Like Daniel, let us pray that God will continue to forgive the church's sin, that he will comfort and strengthen us, that he will keep us bold and courageous, but also humble and submissive. Let us pray that our children and grandchildren are given strength from above to withstand the persecution of tomorrow. Let us pray that they, like Daniel and his friends, are granted God's wisdom to understand the times and know what the church should do. Above all, let us pray as Jesus did that those after us will be one in Christ so that the world will believe on him, even as they put his servants to death (John 17:21). Let us pray that Christ is glorified always, whether in life or in death (Phil. 1:20).

CONCLUSION

This chapter is among the most difficult passages in the Bible. But for all its confusion and ambiguity, it clearly illustrates God's attitude toward sin and his resolve to deliver his people from it. God does not save us from our sins so that we will feel better about them. Rather, God saves us from sin that we might learn to hate it as much as he does. In Christ death and resurrection, God addressed sin once and for all. Rather than the end of time, Dan. 9 has to do with the deliverance only Jesus can offer to those who believe and obey.

QUESTIONS FOR REFLECTION

1. Why did Daniel decide to study from Jeremiah?

2. Describe Daniel's emotions concerning Israel's unfaithfulness.

3. What reasoning did Daniel use in asking God to restore the Jews back to Jerusalem?

4. According to Gabriel, what were the six goals of the "seventy weeks"?

5. According to the New Testament, how did Jesus achieve all six of these goals?

QUESTIONS FOR DISCUSSION

1. Does your church pray fervently for God's people, present and future, as Daniel did? If yes, how? If no, why not?

2. In his prayer, Daniel said that Israel had no right to God's grace. Why is this an important fact to rehearse in prayer?

3. At the end of his prayer, Daniel asked God to act for the glory of his own Name. Why is it important that we remember this?

4. Does your church take sin as seriously as Daniel did? If not, why? Be honest and candid in your answer.

5. For all of its confusing details, what do you consider to be the main point of this chapter?

11

THE VISION
DANIEL 10

Objective: To encourage Christians in their spiritual war against the forces of darkness through prayer and devotion to God

INTRODUCTION

The tenth chapter of Daniel begins its final section. In this culminating vision, Daniel is given a glimpse behind the curtain that shrouds the spiritual realm from us mortals. He is told of future events, happenings that will lead to the triumph of God's people. At the time of this vision, Daniel was in his late 80s, and the experience took a toll on his body. Only after he was strengthened and encouraged could he bear the vision.

Daniel 10 is an encouraging chapter that reminds us that there are spiritual battles ongoing that remain unseen, yet the God of heaven is in control, foretelling his ultimate triumph over the forces of evil. Though it's hard to believe, our actions here on earth have the ability to effect change in the spiritual realm. In Dan. 10, Daniel is told that his devotion to God has elicited a heavenly response and has aided the forces of God in their battle against evil.

EXAMINATION

Read Daniel 10:1-9. This final vision came to Daniel in Cyrus' third year (536 B.C.), and it would prove to be a massive one, characterized by some of the most specific predictions in Scripture. This vision was a lengthy one about a major war in both the spiritual and physical realms. When the vision came, Daniel had been fasting and praying for three weeks. He had suspended the use of lotions, which were applied in hot, dry climates as a sort of deodorant; thus, they were not used during periods of mourning. Daniel was grieving perhaps because of a premonition of the difficulties facing the Jews in Jerusalem. The foundation of the second Temple would be laid in April 536, but the project would be quickly suspended due to the Samaritans' intense opposition (Ezra 3:8, 10; 4:4-5).

A couple of days before, on Nisan 24 (early April), Daniel saw a "man" standing on the banks of the Tigris River. The description of this "man" (vv. 5-6) is a majestic one. Fine clothes such as a priest would wear, a golden belt, a body of beryl (a yellowish gemstone thought to have come from Spain), a face like lightening, eyes like torches, limbs like bronze, and a voice like a stadium crowd—this is almost identical to the description of Jesus that John gave (Rev. 1:13-15). Only Daniel could see this "man," but his companions were frightened nonetheless and ran away. We are left with the image of Daniel fainting facedown as if paralyzed with fear.

Who is this "man" in Dan. 10? Some scholars take him to be the pre-incarnate Christ. The parallels between the appearance of this "man" in Dan. 10 and the vision of Jesus in Rev. 1 are too striking to ignore. This figure certainly inspired more terror in Daniel than had Gabriel (cf. 8:16; 9:21). Identifying this divine messenger with God would explain why his appearance affected Daniel as it did. The Lord often appeared to his servants in human form at pivotal moments in the scheme of redemption.

Daniel 10:10-21. Daniel was revived and helped to his hands and knees. This mysterious "man" bade him to stand since he had been sent to inform Daniel of why his prayer had not been answered. This divine messenger had been dispatched to answer Daniel's petition as soon as he had begun praying, but "the prince of the Persian kingdom" (v. 13 NIV) had resisted this messenger and delayed him for three weeks. We aren't told specifically how or why the delay was successful, but this prince may have been behind the earthly opposition to the Temple's restoration in Jerusalem. The divine messenger had appeared now only because Michael, the guardian archangel of Israel, had come to his aid. The dark powers knew if this "man's" mission were successful, not only would Daniel (also Israel and the church) be encouraged by the vision, but once the vision was delivered, the events were sure to come to pass.

Twice in this passage, Daniel is said to be "greatly loved" (vv. 11, 19) by God. But due to his advanced age, his recent fast, or the intensity of this vision (arguably a little of all three), Daniel complained it was too much for him. One like "the children of men" called Daniel to have courage and touched him on the lips to strengthen him. Now prepared both spiritually and physically to receive the vision, Daniel was given a startling peek behind the curtain into the spiritual realm. This "man" informed Daniel that he was returning to the fray against the princes of Persia and Greece, with only Michael as his comrade-in-arms.

Having encouraged Daniel, the messenger commenced to relate to the prophet "what is inscribed in the book of truth" (v. 21). The "writing of truth" indicates the foreknowledge of God. He perceives all things, "declaring the end from the beginning and from ancient times things not yet done" (Isa. 46:10). That which God foreknows is certain to take place. Daniel could have confidence that the events that he recorded would come to pass.

APPLICATION

Open Your Eyes. Scripture is clear that God's people are engaged in war; however, this war is not merely physical (cf. Eph. 6:12). While we are physical beings who inhabit a physical realm, we must never forget that spiritual forces exist also. God is a spirit (John 4:24), and his angels are spiritual beings (Heb. 1:14). Even in our struggles against ungodly family members, hostile neighbors, and arrogant superiors, much is at stake spiritually. The kingdom of Christ is not of this world (John 18:36). If we are to be victorious, we must remember that our world is a combination of forces seen and unseen.

Pray with Power. How are we to engage in spiritual warfare? From a survey of New Testament teaching, it seems one of our primary weapons is prayer. In prayer, we not only align our priorities with God's, but we also lend a mysterious hand to angels fighting on our behalf. Prayer becomes a rather formidable weapon when we petition for our enemies to repent and be forgiven. "The prayer of a righteous person has great power as it is working" (Jas. 5:16). Evidently, Daniel's prayers played an important part in the battle between the "man" and the prince of Persia. It's not surprising, therefore, that the apostle Paul placed primacy on prayer (1 Tim. 2:1). Whenever God's people find themselves living in a culture hostile to faith and godliness, the church should devote more time to sincere prayer. Otherwise, we should not be surprised if we become casualties in this struggle against the dark powers.

CONCLUSION

Apparently, a struggle had been taking place in the spiritual realm between the angels and the demon of Persia, perhaps for the soul of Cyrus around the time he allowed the Jews to return to Jerusalem (cf. 11:1; Ezra 1:1). It wouldn't be long before this struggle would also involve the demon of Greece; much of Dan. 11 concerns Israel during the days of the Greek Empire. Bizarre as it sounds, the divine messenger seemed thankful for Daniel's persistent prayer since only Michael was by the messenger's side. Paul was adamant that the church's war is not with physical powers, but with evil, spiritual powers (Eph. 6:12); the armor and weapons of this war belong not to the world (2 Cor. 10:3-4), but to God: truth, righteousness, faith, salvation, the gospel, and the Word (Eph. 6:14-17). Paul then exhorted us to wage spiritual warfare by "praying at all times in the Spirit, with all prayer and supplication. To that end keep alert with all perseverance, making supplication for all the saints" (Eph. 6:18; cf. Luke 18:1).

QUESTIONS FOR REFLECTION

1. Why was Daniel fasting?

2. How does Daniel describe the "man" he saw in this vision?

3. Who delayed the divine messenger from responding to Daniel's prayer?

4. What is indicated by the "writing of truth" mentioned by the messenger?

5. What does this passage say about the connection or parallel between the spiritual and physical realms?

QUESTIONS FOR DISCUSSION

1. Fasting isn't as prevalent today as it was during the Old and New Testaments. Why should Christians fast?

2. Who do you believe the "man" of Dan. 10 to be? Why?

3. Why was Daniel greatly beloved?

4. How did the spiritual beings—the princes of Persia, Greece, and Israel—influence events occurring in the physical world?

5. If God knows the future, how can prayer change the future?

6. What must Daniel have thought when he learned what his prayers had accomplished?

12

THE SCRIPT

DANIEL 11

Objective: To affirm God's forknowledge of the future, and thus to inspire trust in him in good times and bad

INTRODUCTION

The prophecy of this chapter is startling in its detail and accuracy; some 130 predictions are made in the first 35 verses. Nowhere else in the Old Testament is so much specific, predictive prophecy found in one place, and the acid test of whether prophecy is from God is if it comes to pass (Deut. 18:20-22). This chapter describes more than 400 years of events that lay in the future from Daniel's perspective; it reads like a historical survey of the period with only names and dates missing. If you aren't a fan of history, this chapter might seem boring to you. But it is important to witness the prophecy's accuracy relative to the way history played out.

The effect of this massive series of prophecies should be the same for us as it was for Daniel and the original readers—if God is great and mighty enough to make known the end from the beginning, then he is worthy of our trust during the darkest seasons of life. God has more than the whole world in his hands—those same hands hold the future as well. We need not fear what lies ahead.

EXAMINATION

Read Daniel 11:1-9. Two hundred years of Persian history are quickly passed over at the outset, but not without mentioning a fourth king, Xerxes I, who was indeed very wealthy and launched a campaign against Greece in 480 B.C. He was slowed considerably by the courageous 300 Spartans at Thermopylae and later defeated (v. 2). Persia and Greece were at odds with one another until the rise of Alexander the Great in 336. Alexander's rule ended in 323 almost as soon as it had begun. Within a few years after his death, all of Alexander's undisputed heirs were assassinated, and his empire was eventually divided among four of his generals (vv. 3-4); two of whom were Seleucus I in Syria ("the king of the north") and Ptolemy I in Egypt ("the king of the south").

Seleucus was initially challenged by another of Alexander's generals, Antigonus I, and was forced to seek asylum in Egypt under Ptolemy. This made Seleucus one of Ptolemy's "princes" for about four years before defeating Antigonus and regaining control over Syria, thus making him "stronger than" Ptolemy (v. 5).

About 75 years after Alexander's death, Ptolemy II offered a peace treaty to the Seleucid ruler, Antiochus II, in the form of his (Ptolemy's) daughter's (Berenice's) hand in marriage. But for this to work, Antiochus had to divorce his current wife, Laodice, and disinherit their two sons. He did so, but Laodice later poisoned Antiochus and arranged for her son, Seleucus II, to murder Berenice and her baby. Seleucus II then inherited the throne (v. 6).

Before the deaths of Antiochus and Berenice, Ptolemy II (Berenice's father) died, bringing Ptolemy III to power. He avenged Berenice's assassination by invading Syria and seizing the capital. Ptolemy returned to Egypt with much plunder, including 40,000 talents of silver and 2,500 idols (vv. 7-8). In 242, Seleucus II retaliated by invading Egypt, but was forced to retreat very quickly (v. 9).

Read Daniel 11:10-19. In 217, Seleucus' son, Antiochus III, met Ptolemy IV in battle at the fortress at Raphia, but Ptolemy was victorious, suffering only 2,200 casualties to Antiochus' 17,000. Palestine subsequently came under the dominion of the Ptolemies (vv. 10-12).

Ptolemy IV died in his 30s in 203 B.C. under suspicious circumstances. Since his son, Ptolemy V, was just six at the time, Agathocles the prime minister was the true ruler, but he became very unpopular. Antiochus III (Syria) and Philip V (Greece) exploited the crisis by defeating the Egyptians in 200. These victories reclaimed Palestine for the Seleucids (v. 13). Two years later, Antiochus III besieged the Egyptian fortress-city of Sidon on the Mediterranean coast, further strengthening his hold of "the glorious land" or Palestine (vv. 15-16).

Meanwhile, Rome was slowly gaining power. In response, Antiochus III allied with the Ptolemies against Rome by giving his daughter, Cleopatra I, as a wife to Ptolemy V, who was only sixteen at the time. The ploy backfired, however, when Cleopatra convinced her husband to ally with Rome against her father (v. 17).

Antiochus III attacked Rome-protected Greece in 192. But the Romans defeated Antiochus in 191 and 190, the latter being a crushing blow to Antiochus. In 189, he signed a treaty with Rome that required him to forfeit twenty hostages (one of them being Antiochus' son, Antiochus IV), submit to Rome as a vassal, and pay a rather large indemnity for being such a headache. This last requirement left Antiochus broke. Two years later, Antiochus was assassinated for plundering a temple in Persia in an effort to pay his bill to Rome (vv. 18-19).

Read Daniel 11:20-28. Seleucus IV inherited the throne when

Antiochus III died, and he sent his prime minister to plunder the Jerusalem Temple treasury for funds to pay the Romans their annual tribute, but a dream scared Seleucus IV into backing down. He did not reign long; instead of dying with his boots on, he was poisoned in 175 (v. 20). Seleucus' brother, Antiochus IV, was returning from Rome when the assassination took place. This, then, is how the infamous Antiochus IV rose to power. He was indeed "a contemptible person," and "royal majesty" (v. 21) technically did not belong to him since Seleucus' son was the rightful heir to the throne. Nonetheless, Antiochus was a master of intrigue (8:23) and seized his throne "by flatteries." He was known to give more lavish gifts to his supporters compared to his predecessors.

Since Persian times, the Jews had been allowed to be ruled by the Torah with the high priest ("the prince of the covenant," v. 22) in charge. Onias III was high priest in Jerusalem when Antiochus IV became king. But Antiochus was committed to spreading Greek culture as much as possible. So he deposed Onias in favor of a non-Levite, Menelaus, who later assassinated Onias (vv. 23-24).

In 170, Antiochus IV attacked Ptolemy VI and defeated him; in the aftermath, he captured much of Egypt (v. 25). Two of Ptolemy's advisors, Eulaeus and Lenaeus, convinced him to flee after Antiochus had seized much of Egypt; they were possibly trying to undermine Ptolemy. Ptolemy did flee, but Antiochus captured him, and Ptolemy's little brother, Ptolemy VII, became king (v. 26). Antiochus attempted to control Egypt from afar by installing Ptolemy VI as a rival against Ptolemy VII (remember that both boys, as sons of Cleopatra I, were Antiochus' nephews), but no sooner had Antiochus started for home than the two brothers buried the hatchet and decided to rule jointly over Egypt (v. 27). Meanwhile, Antiochus stopped to plunder the Jerusalem Temple on his way home because he was short of funds (v. 28).

Read Daniel 11:29-35. In 168, Antiochus IV attacked Egypt again, furious that his nephews had allied against him. Things didn't go so well for Antiochus this time since the brothers appealed to Rome for help. In what must have been an epic showdown, the Roman envoy confronted Antiochus at Alexandria and gave him an ultimatum to return home or face Rome's wrath. Antiochus hemmed and hawed, but his stalling didn't work—the Roman envoy drew a circle around Antiochus and ordered him not to step out until he had answered the ultimatum. Antiochus, embarrassed and angry, nonetheless capitulated (vv. 29-30).

Somehow, a rumor that Antiochus had died in Egypt made its way to Jerusalem, and his puppet high priest, Menelaus, was assassinated. On his way home, Antiochus heard about it and suspected a revolt was taking place. Still smarting over being humiliated by Rome at Alexandria, Antiochus' army massacred 80,000 men, women, and children in Jerusalem on the Sabbath. Antiochus also stationed troops in a citadel near the Temple, an act of sacrilege in the minds of God's people. He also banned sacrifices and all Temple worship. Other religious observances so critical to the Law and Jewish identity (e.g. Sabbath, circumcision, kosher laws) were also prohibited. Torah scrolls were publicly burned. The worst of it came in December 167 when Antiochus "erected a desolating sacrilege on the altar of burnt offering" (1 Macc. 1:54). Specifically, he sacrificed a pig to Zeus on the holy altar (vv. 30-31).

There were varied responses to Antiochus' antics. Some, no doubt due to Antiochus' slick politics, went along with everything, turning their back on the Law of Moses and the covenant. But other Jews resisted, and some of those quite violently, eventually culminating in the Maccabean revolt (vv. 32-35). Notice how the divine messenger mentions "the wise" vv. 33, 35. He was referring to those Jews who knew the Scriptures and were faithful to the Lord. Unlike their unfaithful countrymen, they were spiritually equipped to face these difficult times because they knew the Word and knew God!

Read Daniel 11:36-45. During this period, it is clear God allowed Antiochus to do almost whatever he wanted, but that included Antiochus adopting the moniker *Theou Epiphanes*, meaning "God manifest" or "God revealed" (v. 36). In many ways, Antiochus diverged from the policies and traditions of his predecessors. While the Seleucids had worshiped Apollo ("the gods of his fathers"), and the Ptolemies had patronized Adonis ("the one beloved by women"), Antiochus promoted the Zeus cult (vv. 37-38). That Antiochus went way too far is seen in how his contemporaries secretly gave him an amended nickname, *Epimanes*, meaning "madman." Despite his blasphemy, the true God of heaven would allow Antiochus to reign "till the indignation is accomplished," a haunting reminder that Antiochus was a scourge against Israel as discipline for her sins (v. 36). But his reign was not indefinite; God always appoints an end to his people's suffering!

Up to v. 40, this chapter has been a striking prediction of what was yet to take place in Daniel's time. Since v. 21, the story has concerned the reign of Antiochus IV, but the final six verses of Dan. 11 do not match anything from Antiochus' life, though there seems to be no identifiable break in the subject of vv. 21-39 and vv. 40-45. We know from secular historians that Antiochus died while in Persia, and from a sudden illness, rather than in battle.

That's why some interpreters claim these final six verses point to an end-times Antichrist figure foreshadowed by Antiochus, perhaps a being equal to the man of lawlessness in 2 Thess. 2 and the beast of Rev. 13. But there is nothing in the text indicating we should skip ahead to the end of time to understand the passage. Other scholars consider vv. 40-45 to be a general review of Antiochus' life, but the phrase "At the time of the end" (v. 40) seems to nix that argument.

Interpreters of yesteryear considered these verses to be about Herod the Great, the Roman Empire, the rise of Islam, or the Catholic papacy. During the height of the Cold War, it was popular to identify Russia with the king of the north, but as you can imagine, few buy into that idea anymore.

In light of so much rampant speculation, it's unwise to interpret the passage literally. There are several ties between vv. 40-45 and the prophecies of Isaiah and Ezekiel that predict the overthrow of Assyria and Babylon. Using language and metaphors of former prophets, the vision might simply be forecasting Antiochus' demise in a non-specific way. If I said, "I'm gonna make you an offer you can't refuse," you wouldn't take me literally, but you'd have a fair idea of what I was getting at if you'd seen *The Godfather*. The same goes for phrases such as "We're not in Kansas anymore," "We'll always have Paris," or "Houston, we have a problem." The language of vv. 40-45 might need to be interpreted in a similar way.

Regardless of who is being discussed in these final six verses, we cannot miss the great climax of the passage—"he shall come to his end." No ruler, no matter how oppressive he might be, can stand against God forever. A detailed account of things to come is intended, not to help us guess what happens next, but to deepen our faith in God. He is in control, he will keep his promises, and he will never forsake us, but will rather be with us until the end (Matt. 28:20).

APPLICATION

The Script of History. There are times when the events of history will seem to have no clear direction or purpose. One nation rises and another falls; one tyrant holds power for a lifetime, while another is deposed after just a few days. But this chapter makes clear that God is in control, even in the most random of circumstances. Remarkably, no one king in Dan. 11 successfully holds power for very long, not even Antiochus IV. The most ambitious and tyrannical of rulers is still held in check by God. Christians know "the rest of the story." Not every detail leading up to the end has been revealed to us, but we have been assured of the final outcome. That's why we can read tomorrow's news with all the tranquility of a sleeping child in its mother's arms. Christians don't know what the future holds, but we know who holds the future. Let us, therefore, confess with Paul: "I know whom I have believed, and I am convinced that he is able to guard until that Day what has been entrusted to me" (2 Tim. 1:12).

The Response of the Wise. In vv. 33, 35, the divine messenger said that "the wise" would suffer hardship during Antiochus' reign of terror "so that they may be refined, purified, and made white," but they would endure and be delivered by God. In v. 33, it is said that they would "make many understand." As God's people living in a hostile environment, we must embrace all suffering as an opportunity to be refined and purified by God (1 Pet. 1:6-7). We must also look to Scripture, not to learn what will happen next, but to understand the times we live in and to discern how God wants us to live. The Bible offers us a lot of comfort and direction in challenging times if we will just read it. And in the extreme cases when we simply don't know what to do, God has graciously promised to grant wisdom to those who seek it (Jas. 1:5).

CONCLUSION

This chapter is filled with specific prophecies about the future from Daniel's perspective. When we compare the prophecies to the historical record, we should be filled with awe and wonder at God's power to foresee the future with such detail. It should also inspire us to trust in God no matter what. He holds the future in his hands, and he will work every event for our good and his glory.

QUESTIONS FOR REFLECTION

1. What purpose did God have in revealing such a specific script for the future to Daniel?

2. As you read Dan. 11 and read this lesson, what truth or fact was impressed upon you the most?

3. How is Antiochus IV described in this chapter? What do we learn here about him that we were not told in Dan. 8?

4. According to vv. 32-35, how were righteous Jews able to successfully resist Antiochus' reign of terror?

5. Though the exact meaning of vv. 40-45 might remain a mystery to us, what is the main point of these verses?

QUESTIONS FOR DISCUSSION

1. What do you think was Daniel's response to the very specific nature of this prophecy. If he could have traveled into the future to see these events play out in real time, what would he have thought?

2. This chapter describes the actions of kings, nations, and armies against one another. Do you believe today's political and international events are following a script that God has foreseen? Why/why not?

3. Why did God allow Antiochus IV to rise to power?

4. What are some film or television phrases that have become ingrained in pop culture? Why might God have used metaphors from past prophets in a similar way to describe the end of Antiochus?

5. What potential events in the future do you fear the most? How are you comforted or encouraged by the fact that God knows the future so intimately and controls it so completely?

13

THE END?

DANIEL 12

Objective: To conclude the book of Daniel and preview the deliverance promised to God's people, the church

INTRODUCTION

The final chapter of Daniel is meant to arouse in us an abiding faith in God's sovereignty and inspire us to trust him completely with everything, especially the future. If God is capable of accurately foretelling both the events of tomorrow and those a hundred years from now, then he is worthy of our trust, no matter the consequences. It's best to trust and obey God; he alone holds the future in his hand.

This chapter is the conclusion to Daniel's final vision. Though much of the text is difficult to unravel, one thing is sure. God promises safety and salvation to those who trust in him. God's people—both Israel and the church—would encounter severe tribulation; nevertheless, God would remain faithful and deliver those who would persevere. God always takes care of his people!

EXAMINATION

Read Daniel 12:1-4. Appropriately, the book of Daniel ends somewhat enigmatically. The beginning of Dan. 12 mentions the rise of the archangel Michael, mixed with a very turbulent period "such as never has been." But Daniel is assured his people, particularly those whose names are in the book of life, will be delivered. The resurrected will shine like stars. Daniel is then told to seal the book until "the time of the end." There is also the cryptic phrase, "Many shall run to and fro, and knowledge shall increase" (v. 4).

These verses do not have to do with the end of time, but nor do they refer to the period of Antiochus. Remember that the vision of Dan. 10-12 concerned Daniel's people, i.e. Israel. It thus seems as if Dan. 12 refers somewhat to Rome's destruction of Jerusalem in A.D. 70, but also to how God delivered his faithful people in the midst of such a difficult period. Jesus described these events as a "great tribulation, such as has not been from the beginning of the world until now, no, and never will be" (Matt. 24:21). If Jesus alluded to Dan. 12 in Matt. 24, how can these verses concern the time of Antiochus exclusively?

During the Maccabean revolt, it was commonly believed that the Jews received divine aid in battle (2 Macc. 10:29-30; 11:6-13; 15:22-27). Whether the archangel Michael gave direct help to God's people then is uncertain, but it's not a stretch to believe that he protected the church at God's direction when Rome came against Jerusalem. Before A.D. 70, Christians abandoned Jerusalem because they remembered Jesus' warning. Rome's wrath only affected those Jews who had rejected Jesus as the Messiah. We must thus adopt a new definition of "God's people." In light of the gospel, it is no longer limited to descendants of Israel, but to all those who are in Christ (Gal. 3:28).

Is the resurrection mentioned in v. 2 the final, bodily resurrection set to occur when Jesus returns? Or is it a spiritual resurrection experienced in the gospel? Scholars are divided on the issue, and the evidence in this passage may be inconclusive. Jesus spoke of the final resurrection using similar language (John 5:28-29), but a few verses earlier, seemed to allude to a spiritual resurrection (John 5:24; cf. Rom. 6:5; Eph. 2:5). It may not matter which resurrection is in view in Dan. 12 since those who are resurrected spiritually with Christ in baptism (Rom. 6:3-6) indeed have the hope of everlasting life where they will shine like stars (vv. 2-3; cf. 1 Cor. 15:41-42; 2 Tim. 4:8).

The command to "shut up the words and seal the book" meant Daniel was to make sure its message was safeguarded. To "seal" a scroll meant to place one's signet ring in hot wax over the scroll's closing as a mark of authenticity. The scroll was then placed in a secure location. Whenever important documents (e.g. legal or financial) were sealed and "shut up" in ancient times, it was to protect the original copy should there ever be a dispute as to its contents (cf. Jer. 32:11, 14). Remember that, when Daniel received this vision, Cyrus had only been reigning a few years, and the events described in Dan. 11 were several centuries in the future. It's no wonder Daniel could not understand these things (v. 8). But by sealing its contents and placing it in a safe place, Daniel's prophetic word could be retrieved as these things came to pass; his claims would be validated, and the people of God would be inspired to continue trusting in the only One who knows the end from the beginning.

In contrast to these saints who sought understanding and encouragement in the Word of God (cf. Rom. 15:4), Daniel is told, "Many shall run to and fro, and knowledge shall increase." This statement is very similar to Amos 8:11-12. In troubled times, whether centuries ago, or in centuries to come, there will be those who seek signs and messages from the Lord, all the while refusing to read what God has so clearly said in Scripture.

Read Daniel 12:5-13. At this point, Daniel noticed two angels on opposite banks of the Tigris, and one of them asked the mysterious "man" of Dan. 10, "How long will it be before these astonishing things are fulfilled?" (v. 6 NIV). The "man" solemnly swore by God himself that the period would last an ambiguous "time, times, and half a time" (v. 7; cf. 7:25). We're given a little more of an idea of when this period would end by the phrase "the shattering of the power of the holy people," i.e. the time when the Jews' power would be broken by Rome's destruction of Jerusalem. This terrible event was punishment for the Jews having rejected Jesus, so the Son of Man dashed "them in pieces like a potter's vessel" (cf. Psa. 2:9-12). When Daniel inquired further, he was told to continue living his life. His visions were drawing to a close.

The divine messenger tells Daniel that 1,290 days would pass between the suspension of Temple worship and the end of the period. But then comes another confusing statement—"Blessed is he who waits and arrives at the 1,335 days" (12:12). Though no one has given a solid or satisfactory explanation of the two time periods mentioned in vv. 11-12, we can be sure that they were meant to be an encouragement to Daniel and to those who would read his vision. God's people have the strength to persevere because their suffering is only temporary and will be crowned with eternal glory. Symbolic or otherwise, the phrase likely has to do with the destruction of Jerusalem. From the time the Romans first appeared at Jerusalem to the final sacrifice being offered in the Temple was about 3½ years. The additional 45 days may be a way of saying, "Soon after the final sacrifice, the period of oppression will be brought to an end. Hold on a little while longer!"

Or, to use Jesus' words, "the one who endures to the end will be saved" (Matt. 24:13).

APPLICATION

God's Word Is Final. Though Daniel's vision was compelling and provided exciting information about Israel's future, many of God's people would continue to search for answers elsewhere. God's command to seal the scroll would ensure that his Word would stand firm, that it was undeniable and unavoidable. Jesus knew many would be deceived into searching for revelation elsewhere, neglecting to trust his words (Matt. 24:23). "They will accumulate for themselves teachers to suit their own passions, and will turn away from listening to the truth and wander off into myths" (2 Tim. 4:3-4). God's Word is not lacking in our day, yet people continue to search for revelation elsewhere. What God has already revealed is sufficient and complete (2 Tim. 3:16-17; 2 Pet. 1:3; Jude 3). New revelation will not be added. We have Christ, Moses, and the prophets. Let us hear them (Luke 16:29).

The Bible & Curiosity. Evidently, Daniel did not know that "curiosity killed the cat." As his vision was drawing to a conclusion, he asked the heavenly messenger for more information (v. 8). Daniel was instructed to continue living his life. The messenger politely told Daniel that he would not be given more specific information. Many of the ancient prophets found themselves in similar positions. They searched their own writings and the writings of others to find information about which they were deeply concerned (1 Pet. 1:11-12). Though Daniel's inquiry hints at something deeper than mere curiosity, we need to be wary of viewing the Bible as a novelty—searching its pages for bits of trivia and information to satisfy our own human desires. Since God's Word is final and sufficient, we have been given all the information that we need (2 Pet. 1:3). We need to be careful to study God's Word appropriately and not mistake the curiosities of the trees for the grandeur of the forest.

God's New Nation. Though much of Daniel's prophecy is concerned with the physical, fleshly nation of Israel, this last vision gives a glimpse of the coming of a new kingdom. Smatterings about this new kingdom are found throughout the entirety of the book. Studying the text from our vantage point reminds us that the church, the beautiful bride of Christ, has forever been concealed in the mind of God. Though we were not a people, now we are the sons of God (1 Pet. 2:10). In Christ, physical heritage means nothing (Gal. 3:28). Jew and Gentile have been united in one body—the church. Though Daniel (and later other inspired writers) could barely conceive of the redemption of the Gentiles, God's message of triumphant grace extended to them. Let us glorify God for a kingdom into which all the nations now flow.

CONCLUSION

This last chapter is a fitting close to the book. Daniel began as a young captive in Babylon, but by the close of the final chapter, he is advanced in age and greatly beloved by God. The Lord blessed him for his devotion, protected him in a lion's den, and preserved him in a distant land. That same God would continue to sustain Daniel's countrymen, and God's Word would continue to stand. Undoubtedly, the final years of Daniel's life brought him peace. The Jews (at least in part) returned to the Promised Land, and the Temple was rebuilt. As we ponder the message of Daniel, we can find that same calm assurance. Regardless of the uncertain future before us, God is still in control and will bring about his purposes in his time.

QUESTIONS FOR REFLECTION

1. According to the messenger, who will shine like stars?

2. Who are God's people today?

3. Why was Daniel told to "shut up the words and seal the book"?

4. How many days would pass between the suspension of Temple worship and the end of the period?

5. Why were Daniel's questions left unanswered?

QUESTIONS FOR DISCUSSION

1. Is the resurrection mentioned in this chapter physical or spiritual? Explain your answer.

2. Why do some reject the Word of God, searching for revelation or direction from the Lord elsewhere?

3. What is meant by "Blessed is he who waits and arrives at the 1,335 days" (12:12)?

4. What difference has studying Daniel made in your life?

PERSONAL NOTES

PERSONAL NOTES

PERSONAL NOTES

PERSONAL NOTES

PERSONAL NOTES

PERSONAL NOTES

PERSONAL NOTES

PERSONAL NOTES

PERSONAL NOTES

PERSONAL NOTES

PERSONAL NOTES

PERSONAL NOTES

PERSONAL NOTES

PERSONAL NOTES

SUGGESTED RESOURCES

Baldwin, Joyce G. *Daniel*. Downers Grove, IL: InterVarsity Press, 1978.

Hailey, Homer. *Commentary on Daniel*. Las Vegas: Nevada Publications, 2001.

Longman, Tremper, III. Daniel. Grand Rapids: Zondervan, 1999.

Whitworth, Michael. *The Derision of Heaven*. Bowie, TX: Start2Finish, 2013.

Young, Edward J. *The Prophecy of Daniel*. Grand Rapids: Eerdmans, 1949.

ABOUT THE AUTHOR

MICHAEL WHITWORTH is the owner of Start2Finish and ministers for the church of Christ in Keller, Texas. He is the author of several books, including the award-winning *The Epic of God* and *The Derision of Heaven*.

He considers M&Ms his brain food and is fond of large Mason jars. In his spare time, Michael loves reading and drinking coffee, watching sports, and spending time with his family and furry golden retriever.

To order additional Bible Studies from Start2Finish, visit start2finish.org/bible-studies, call (888) 978-3850, or ask for them at your favorite Christian bookstore.

Also available for Kindle, Nook, & iBooks.

www.ingramcontent.com/pod-product-compliance
Lightning Source LLC
Chambersburg PA
CBHW071738080526
44588CB00013B/2078